CW00502357

ALLEN ARNOLD

CHAOS CAN'T

Overcome What
Comes Against You
in This Shaken World

Printed in the United States of America

ISBN: 978-0-578-76274-6 (print)

First Edition

10 9 8 7 6 5 4 3 2 1

To Bart Hansen

A wise sage and good friend.
You have shown me—through
your life and through countless
conversations over cigars—
that chaos can't win.
You are a man of great adventure...
and even greater love.

"But when the world is, indeed,
in chaos, then an affirmation of
cosmos becomes essential."

—Madeleine L'Engle

I see that the LORD
is always with me.
I will not be shaken,
for he is right beside me.
(Acts 2:25 NLT)

CONTENTS

Advance Words for This Journey

Just a few years ago, it was rare to hear the word *chaos* in most conversations. Back then, when I was asked what I was writing about and I responded, "chaos," people would nod politely and then quickly try to exit. Or change the topic to something . . . more topical.

Has that ever changed.

Now chaos is invading every area of our lives . . . and conversations.

It is relentless. It is unquenchable. It refuses to be contained. It seeks to devour and destroy. To replace order with disorder like a virus trying to infect everyone and everything. But it doesn't just appear in big, generic ways.

Chaos also comes at us in unique, almost customized, ways. It's as if it knows us and infuses our hopes and dreams with fear in the places we are most vulnerable.

So what is chaos really? And when it hits, how should we respond?

You won't find the answers on the nightly news or social media. They report chaos, stir fear, and take sides... but have no clue for a cure. Because they are looking in the wrong places. That's why our search takes a refreshingly different approach.

In our quest for answers, God will be our sage. Scripture will be our guide. And through this mythic yet practical journey into the past—and the future—you will discover what's really going on. We often blame ourselves for the problems and chaos in life. But what if the problem isn't primarily you? Sure, we all do dumb things and make mistakes. In that sense, we can sabotage our own life. But if there's more at play, wouldn't it be helpful to know what that is?

What overwhelms you didn't start with you, but you can overcome it.

Don't wait for things to calm down before starting this journey. There will never be the perfect moment to read about defeating chaos. Putting it off just means you'll be stuck trying the same things that haven't worked the next time chaos strikes. Even if you're in the middle of a storm, try to find a quiet place and begin.

I've done my best to make this the kind of book you can finish in several hours or perhaps over a weekend. Each chapter is just a few pages. Big ideas in bite-size pieces. But the order matters, so don't jump ahead.

You may feel like you're in over your head at this moment. That little in your life makes sense.

Stay hopeful. I truly believe this message will prove a lifeline for you. It has for me.

1

THE LAST SNOW GLOBE

Beast on Island

There was once a small island in the Mediterranean Sea. It was so tiny that most folks didn't even know it existed.

It didn't produce things the world thought was amazing.

But a family on the island did create something unique.

They made snow globes unlike any others.

Most snow globes are made to be shaken. The white particles fill the sphere in a chaotic swirl. But no matter how hard these globes were shaken, what was inside remained calm.

The shaken world wasn't sure what to make of such an odd creation, so it ignored them.

Where other snow globes had fake snow, these contained crystals of ice that never melted but were filled with light. The glistening light and ice seemed to change colors as they danced within the globe. Some of the colors were so new they didn't yet have a name.

The secret to these snow globes was the water. It originated from a cave in the middle of the island. In this cave was a magnificent waterfall that sparkled with light. It flowed day and night, a mighty rush of living water infused with lights and colors.

The cave needed no outside light. The waterfall was so bright that it illuminated the entire cave. The family made their hand-crafted globes in the cave. Surrounded by the colorful living water, it was an atmosphere of joy, laughter, and love.

You'd think the way the waterfall sparkled and lit up the dark cave, everyone would be drawn to it. But most people on the island were afraid to enter the cave. Not because of the living water but because of the words on the rocky ledge right above the waterfall.

On that ledge sat numerous blocks of stone. A letter was carved into each stone. Together, the blocks of stone spelled out:

B E A S T O N I S

Though the last several blocks had fallen off the ledge, everyone could fill in the blanks.

B E A S T O N I S L A N D

No one knew when those words first appeared in the cave, or who put them there. Over time, people began to believe the warning had been there since the island came into existence.

The words struck fear in their hearts. Because no matter how beautiful the living water was, the warning above it was all people remembered.

And from the warning grew a legend.

That all was hopeless. That ultimately the beast on the island would steal, kill, and destroy all that was good. After all, what power could living water have against a raging beast?

The family who made the snow globes ignored the

letters on the ledge, focusing instead on the waterfall.

But others focused on the beast. Some spent their time hiding from it. Or trying to track it. Some locked their doors and turned off their lights, hoping it would leave them alone.

As the fear on the island grew, the rushing waterfall began to slow. Then one day, it quit flowing all together.

Without the living water, the family could no longer make the snow globes. They sold all they had, except for the one that their daughter, Elena, kept.

It was the last snow globe.

Without the sparkling waterfall to light the cave, the family quit coming to work. Their hearts were too heavy. Their eyes now only saw the warning above the place living water used to flow.

But Elena was still drawn to the cave. She believed in the water more than in the warning.

One day, she noticed blocks of stone behind where the waterfall used to flow. They must have fallen off the ledge in the past, hidden from sight as long as the rushing water was present. But not now.

The girl looked at the blocks on the ground. Then up to the ones on the ledge. There should be four blocks but curiously, there were only three. And the letters on them weren't the ones needed to complete the word *island*.

She was confused. But she had an idea.

Maybe the letters above the waterfall had never spelled the right words. What if they had been used in a way they were never meant to be?

The rocky ledge was twenty feet high. She decided to carry the stone blocks back up to the ledge, one at a time.

Elena carefully climbed the rocky steps and added one block. Then the next. Finally the last.

Out of breath, she paused after adding the last one. She looked not at what the letters had been made to spell. But at what they could say.

She decided to re-create it. So the girl added new spaces to the letters to form new words. And smiled.

Climbing down, she was filled with hope.

The living water had made the island a place of peace. But as the fear of the warning grew, the water slowed. What if she could somehow replace the fear of a beast with the hope of love?

But how could she do that without the waterfall?

Elena sighed and put her hands in her pocket. She felt something round in one of the pockets. It was her snow globe. The last snow globe.

She held it high, like a beacon of light. It lit up the cave. Colors danced on the stone walls as light radiated from the crystals and water inside.

Then she brought the globe close to her face. And remembered.

The globe had living water in it.

What if she let it out? It wasn't much, but what if it was enough?

She looked at the new message on the ledge, the one she had remade, and knew what she had to do.

Elena tightened her grip on the snow globe and then threw it at the dry wall. The wall that used to be hidden by the magnificent waterfall. The glass shattered into countless shards. And the water that had been within the globe drizzled down the wall.

But the drops of water then became a sheet of water.

Then a flow of water. Apparently a little living water goes a long way. Soon, the waterfall was rushing again.

Filled with joy, the girl ran out to share the good news.

But before she did, she glanced back at the words on the ledge above the waterfall.

The three new blocks made all the difference. One bore the letter D. One a letter H. And the third, an E.

What had said B E A S T   O N   I S was now recreated to say what it always meant to say.

It was an invitation to live expectantly. To drink deep from the living water. To . . .

B E   A S T O N I S H E D

2

SHAKEN AND OVERWHELMED

Fear was never the intended
message for our lives—
nor does it get the last word.

The Invitation

Be astonished.

I hope the simple story of "The Last Snow Globe" is a powerful reminder that fear was never the intended message for our lives—nor does it get the last word.

Like Elena, we live on an island of sorts. Let's call it a globe. And our globe is being shaken harder and harder by the forces of chaos. As it's shaken, so are we.

The snow globe on the front cover of this book reflects our shaken world. The more chaotic it is, the more shook-up everyone in it tends to become. It's like trying to do everyday life in a continuous earthquake. Or in a swirling snowstorm. It's hard to gain our bearings. To think straight. To see what's really going on.

Did you notice how that globe is unlike the last snow globe? That's because I wanted to provide you with two radically different images as we begin.

Elena's snow globe is a source of calm, filled with living water. The external chaos can't get inside it. But those on the island didn't know what to do with a snow globe—or a hope—that couldn't be shaken. Our world is much the same. Yet there is a way for us to keep our hearts calm no matter how shaken everything around us becomes.

We're about to embark on a journey. The primary focus of it isn't actually chaos. The point isn't to dwell on the havoc in our lives, get used to it, or tremble in fear over the "beast on island." Each of us, in our own ways, has done enough of that. It doesn't work.

The goal is to turn our focus on God. From that place, we can overcome what comes against us. We can actively slow its spread by not letting it into our hearts, homes, dreams, relationships, or areas of gifting. We can be unshaken overcomers.

This is a defiant message of hope. It's time for us to fill the empty, void places around us with beauty, light, and order.

This badly shaken world is in desperate need of that. God has provided a way for us to experience more peace and to then usher it into the places we live and work and play.

This is your invitation, like Elena's, to live expectantly. To drink deep from the living water. And to be astonished.

Chaos—
A New Definition

Before we go further, let's define what we mean by chaos.

Dictionary.com describes it this way:

> *A state of utter confusion or disorder.*

That's a start. We all can relate to the sensation of being confused and disoriented at times. But the definition vastly understates the impact of chaos.

Back in my high school math class, I spent quite a bit of time in "a state of utter confusion." But I wasn't experiencing chaos. I feel a sense of disorder most Monday mornings. But that's not chaos either.

Chaos is more severe and costly. Let me propose a new definition for the purposes of our journey:

> *Chaos is a destructive, fear-based force that prevents you from fully living. The ways it comes against you—large and small—are often intensely personal strikes meant to leave you empty.*

That feels a little more like what's coming against me . . . and probably you.

With that definition in hand, let me share a bit more about this journey we're taking.

Chaos is a destructive, fear-based force that prevents you from fully living. The ways it comes against you—large and small—are often intensely personal strikes meant to leave you empty.

Stepping into the Unknown

This book began with my journey for answers. In many ways, it follows the trajectory of the traditional hero's journey.

Let me be quick to say I'm not the hero of this journey. Whether we realize it or not, God is the deepest longing of all our searches, the hero of every quest for more life.

The unexpected turns that we'll encounter aren't a surprise to God. He regularly invites us into the new and unknown. What we can miss is how his invitations are often initiations. God prepares us for coming opportunities by showing us how to master things beyond our current abilities. We'll never be ready for what's next as long as we're determined to hold tightly to the now.

Richard Niebuhr said, "Pilgrims are poets who create by taking journeys." Initiation is in the DNA of every hero's journey. If you're not familiar with the term, it was coined by literature professor Joseph Campbell in 1949. It refers to a mythic cycle that the protagonist of practically every story follows, whether *Star Wars, The Matrix, Beauty and the Beast*, or *Lord of the Rings*.

There are countless variations, but at a base level, every hero's journey involves an ordinary person choosing to step from the known to the unknown. Doing so requires the help of a sage, an onslaught of challenges, confrontation with the abyss where all seems lost (at the midpoint of the journey), discovering gifts and powers, and ultimately overcoming through some form of death and rebirth. The hero's journey rings true for characters in a story because these same stages are true for the stories we are living. These journeys create a change in us. We begin seeing life one way, but by the last mile, we're no longer the same. We don't just arrive somewhere new. We arrive a different person, transformed by the journey.

It always begins with a tug toward the unknown. It did for me. I was just trying to get through my days. But as the chaos increased, I could feel the negative impact on my heart and my art, on who I am and what I do. I knew chaos was trying to keep me imprisoned, numb to my true calling.

I'm reminded of this quote from the thirteenth-century Persian poet Hafiz: "The small man builds cages for everyone he knows—while the Sage, who has to duck his head when the moon is low, keeps dropping keys all night long for the beautiful, rowdy prisoners."

Chaos rages as God relentlessly drops keys for those the enemy tries to keep captive. Once we are awakened and set free, we can't help but join God in offering light and life to others.

Eventually, I had enough. God dropped me a key and invited me into more. So I set out—with him—for answers.

I'll admit, part of my motive was a deep desire to defeat chaos. Not singlehandedly, like King Arthur slaying the dragon. Though that would be cool. Rather, I wanted to defeat it in my realm. For me and those I love. I wanted my heart—and my creativity—back.

That was more than enough motivation to get me started.

I quickly found myself in way over my head. But that's okay. Unless you choose to stay forever in a small story, you have to undertake adventures where you're no longer the expert. That's why these journeys require a sage.

On this quest, God is our sage. Why do we need his wisdom on this topic when there are countless teachings on how to bring more calm to our lives? Because no one has ever responded better to chaos than God, Jesus, and the Spirit. Nor does any human have the eternal understanding of what's really going on.

"The small man builds cages for everyone he knows—while the Sage, who has to duck his head when the moon is low, keeps dropping keys all night long for the beautiful, rowdy prisoners."

—*Hafiz*

What We're After

My hope is that this quest will reveal:

- why chaos hits in such personal ways;
- how to not let the swirling outside chaos . . . within;
- the possible origin of chaos;
- how to counter fear with love;
- why your creativity matters more than you imagine; and
- 11 ways to restore your dreams and renew your surroundings.

I enter into this as an explorer, not as an expert. I'm not always sure where the next turn is but am confident the journey is a worthy one. As Henry Nouwen says, "Answers before questions do harm to the soul." Theologians smarter than I have spent thousands of years debating many of the things we'll consider. Yet none can be definitive, because none were there at creation. They're trying to make sense of things. As are we.

I'm inviting you to follow me in this journey of discovery. Along the way, I'll do my best to ask good questions and then follow them as far as I can. I'm not a theologian. I'm simply a man who has discovered and accepted God's wild invitation to do life actively with him. That's how I'm approaching this. As a shared adventure. One with huge implications for how we interpret our lives and hold on to our dreams.

My hope is you'll also embrace a sense of expectancy, curiosity, and childlike wonder. If you disagree with a point or two, that's okay. No human has all the answers. Not everything can be diagrammed into a nice chart. No matter how we wish otherwise, eternal questions and the mysteries of God simply don't work that way. God loves it when we seek after him and his ways.

> But without faith it is impossible to please Him, for he who comes to God must believe that He is, and that He is a rewarder of those who diligently seek Him. (Hebrews 11:6 NKJV)

Diligently seeking is what we're doing here. My hunch is if we trust God to guide us, we can better understand the cause of chaos and move to the cure.

Before we get started, I want to offer you some hope:

- The Creator is never surprised or worried about chaos.
- God created you for such a time as this. You can overcome chaos.
- Neither the storms nor the scars get the final word. God does.

Yes, in this moment, chaos can do some real damage. But it can't overpower God. There is a way to overcome what comes against you.

It is possible to live chaos-free in a world filled with chaos. That's what we're after.

How Are You Doing?

Imagine you're sitting around a campfire deep in the middle of a calm forest. You're in a small circle of fellow travelers. The faces are peaceful yet there's a shared intensity. Everyone here has lost something to chaos. And has a desire to overcome it.

The logs in the fire pop and crackle. It's not a time for small talk. It's a moment to look up at the shimmering stars—as well as deep into your heart.

Why did you pick up this book? What is it you hope for this journey?

Chaos comes in a variety of sizes and flavors. It hits in ways we never saw coming. It affects our health, finances, marriage, friendships, faith, family, and dreams. The trail of devastation can result in the loss of a job, the loss of hope, the loss of patience, or even the loss of life.

After numerous encounters, we develop a low-level dread of the next news alert, the bill in the mail, or even what tomorrow holds. Just getting through the day becomes our goal.

So let's name the things you're struggling with in this season. What chaos is swirling in your world? What is being lost or stolen because of it? Write your answers in the space on the next page. Naming something is a way to show it matters, and this matters immensely.

Take a moment to name the things you're struggling with in this season. What chaos is swirling in your world? What is being lost or stolen because of it?

There's no prize for the least or most chaotic experiences. Nor does experience make experts in how to overcome it. So don't get sidetracked. The goal is to gain true freedom from chaos while having compassion *for*—but not comparison *to*—others who are struggling.

Chaos looks and impacts each of us differently. Some is global. There are natural disasters, wars and rumors of wars, viruses, violence, social unrest, self-serving politicians, false prophets, and economic collapse. Some hits far closer to home in the form of cancer or depression. Facing life without a loved one. Financial struggles. A toxic relationship with a boss, spouse, child, or parent. Maybe your chaos is the nonstop to-do list that leaves no time for rest or soul care.

You may be facing chaos on several fronts at once. If you're in a rare reprieve, I'm happy for you. But I'm also here to tell you it won't last. We don't live in paradise.

Chaos hits each of us differently. Yet curiously, it seeks the same thing from each of us. Let's see why.

Unless you choose to stay forever
in a small story, you have to
undertake adventures where
you're no longer the expert.

The Toll It Takes

It's helpful to note how chaos usually begins. Almost always, it starts with an external event that tries to move internally.

You get a panicked call from your friend. A diagnosis from your doctor. A past-due bill you thought you'd paid. An inflammatory comment on social media.

That external situation snags you in its vortex as it accelerates. Then that chaotic swirling tries to get inside your head and your heart.

To cope, we find ways to ignore, numb, or medicate the craziness. We're desperate for relief.

Yet it never seems to come. Not really. The toll chaos takes on our lives is catastrophic. It tries to infuse us with fear, shut down our heart, steal our hope, destroy our dreams, and erode our creativity. It affects us physically, mentally, emotionally, relationally, and spiritually.

I'm sorry for what it has cost you. Though I've never walked in your shoes, I hope this message can offer hope in the midst of your storms.

I was being taken out on multiple fronts. As a writer, I showed up at my keyboard. But the words didn't come. A void was overtaking my imagination. It was like my creativity was freefalling into a huge hole.

I'm not alone on that front. I coach a lot of creative individuals and groups. They have experienced the same thing. Even though they have deep passions, in times of chaos they lose interest in their pursuits. Their focus wanes.

I tried everything to escape chaos. I ignored it, hoping it would go away. If only. I attempted to control it, which just made my world grow smaller. I pretended it didn't affect me, which wasn't true—and later caused me to feel both hopeless and foolish. I hunkered down to wait it out, but passivity can't overcome the storms of life.

What do you do when everything hits the fan? Who do you become? I'm guessing you've tried various ways to manage or deal with the havoc.

Let's expose unhelpful behaviors by naming them.

Typical Reactions to Chaos

Though chaos affects each of us in uniquely personal ways, our reactions to it aren't all that unique. See if you can identify with one or more of the following reactions.

1. We decide to wait it out, hoping to get back to our dreams and plans once things return to normal. But notice what's happening. We're waiting for chaos to end, waiting for calm to return. Passivity is not the antidote.

2. We deny it's a big deal. Things may not be great, but they could be worse. Maybe this is just the new normal. So we keep our eyes—and our hopes—low.

3. We try to decrease chaos by increasing our control of people and situations. But eliminating risk requires us to shrink our world and suffocate those around us with our fear-based demands. The only thing that doesn't shrink is the chaos.

4. We wage war with chaos, determined to fight fire with fire. But it's never a good idea to try to out-chaos chaos. We can't defeat something by

becoming more like it.

5. We seek to profit from it. This is the most disgraceful of all options. Chaos isn't looking for partners. It will use you for a time, then devour you. We "sow the wind and reap the whirlwind" (Hosea 8:7 NIV).

Any of these sound familiar? Ultimately, each response falls short and makes us an easier target for chaos. These options wear us out and let us down. Spun up and worn out, we lick our wounds and shrug our shoulders. We go numb or give in. Broken and bitter, we accept the raging storms as part of life, like an unwanted house guest who barges in and takes over our home. But what can we do?

Perhaps a more sobering questions is why do we keep doing what isn't working?

For me, my exercise in futility started with a faulty assumption. I woke each day expecting everything to go as it should. The storm always caught me off guard. Rather than being ready for it, I was on the defensive. And found myself responding in the typical unhelpful ways.

I was fighting a losing game. Until God used chocolate to show me what was going on.

Though chaos affects each of us
in uniquely personal ways, our
reactions to it aren't all that unique.

In my life, I tried to deal with chaos
one bite at a time.
As long as it came in regularly
spaced intervals and in small doses,
I thought I could handle it.

But chaos isn't playing a game.
It's playing for keeps.

Fighting a Losing Game

We can all use a little more laughter in this shaken world. Few modern sitcoms bring me as much laughter as the classic *I Love Lucy* series.

One of the most popular episodes was the Season 2 premiere titled "Job Switching." In it, Lucy and her best friend, Ethel, take a job working at a chocolate factory. Their duties seem pretty simple. All they have to do is stand side-by-side and wrap bite-size pieces of chocolate as they roll down the assembly line.

If one gets through unwrapped, they'll be fired. But the conveyor belt is going so slow it's a piece of cake. Lucy says, "This is easy." Ethel agrees. "Yeah, we can handle this okay."

Then things begin to change. It takes them a moment to realize it, but the conveyor belt is gradually speeding up. So they go faster. Still in control. But as the belt accelerates, they fall behind. You can see the panic in their eyes as they realize they can't keep up.

Calm goes to chaos as Lucy remarks to Ethel, "I think we're fighting a losing game."

Suddenly the conveyer belt stops. Unwrapped chocolate is everywhere. As the foreman is about to enter their area, they realize they have to hide the evidence of their inability to keep up. So they stuff the candy in their pockets, shirts, hats, and mouths.

The foreman enters, looks at the empty conveyor belt, and nods her approval. "Fine. You're doing splendidly," she announces. Then she shouts to the person operating the belt, "Speed it up a little!"

Lucy and Ethel, mouths full of chocolate, realize pretending everything is okay isn't actually helpful. Hiding their inability to keep up has led to even more chaos.

In my life, I tried to deal with chaos one bite at a time. As long as it came in regularly spaced intervals and in small doses, I thought I could handle it. Though I tried to hold it together for many years, chaos was winning. It was causing me to lose my hope and my temper. Then it sped up, and the stakes got even higher.

Like Lucy and Ethel, I realized I was fighting a losing game. Perhaps you are as well.

But chaos isn't playing a game. It's playing for keeps. And it's speeding up.

Whatever the storm is—
it begins outside of you.
But it doesn't want to stay outside.
It's looking to get in.
Into your head. Into your heart.

Your thoughts are the door
that chaos will use to enter
your heart and mind.
The longer you stay in this mindset,
the wider you open the door.

The First Thing Chaos Wants

It wants in.

Whatever the storm is—it begins outside of you. But it doesn't want to stay outside. It's looking to get in. Into your head. Into your heart.

Notice this: the fact that it wants in means it can't get in without your permission. Someone can knock on your front door. But you choose whether to let him into your home. You'd never let a stranger in if you sensed they wanted to do harm.

Yet we do that all the time with chaos. We let it in.

Consider the disciple Peter when he was in the boat with Jesus. He desperately wanted to walk on water. He initiated the process. But then he shifted his gaze from Jesus before him to the chaos below him. Once Peter let chaos in, he started to sink.

> Jesus didn't hesitate. He reached down and grabbed his hand. Then he said, "Faint-heart, what got into you?" (Matthew 14:31 MSG)

Did you catch what Jesus asked? "What got into you?" In other words, it wasn't Peter but the fear he let in.

In so many things in our lives, it's not us but what we let in. Something happens at work or with your finances.

Perhaps it's a health issue. Or a crisis with one of your children. Maybe you're dealing with all these categories simultaneously. These are the external issues swirling around you. But they remain outside of you unless or until you let them in.

How does it look to let chaos in? It usually begins with unhelpful self-talk. We entertain thoughts like:

"How much can one person handle?"
"Why is it up to me to solve everyone else's problems?"
"Nothing is ever going to change."
"The world is a scary place."
"There's never enough time."
"There's never enough money."
"I'm all on my own."
"Life isn't fair. I always get the raw end of the deal."

This internal monologue never leads anywhere helpful. It weakens your resolve as you start to believe a false interpretation of what's going on. If you embrace these fear-based thoughts, it will change you. And not for the better.

Your thoughts are the door that chaos will use to enter your heart and mind. The longer you stay in this mindset, the wider you open the door.

Rolling Your Window Down in a Car Wash

A while back, my wife pointed out something no one wants to hear. She was incredibly kind, but her words packed a punch. "Allen, you're fine when things are calm. But you don't do so well when chaos hits."

Ouch.

I wanted to challenge her observation. But I knew she was right.

The pattern was familiar to us both. Chaos would start with an external event. Someone was running late. Something broke down. Somebody was angry. Whatever the outside storm was, it came out of nowhere and was intense.

Like rolling down my window in a car wash, I would let the storm inside of me. Who would do that on purpose? The spraying water, the colored foam, the squirting liquids were never meant to get inside your vehicle or on you. Imagine the damage all that would do to your clothes, your hair, your eyes, the electronics and upholstery.

You go through a car wash. But you don't let the car wash into your car.

With God, we can enter the chaos without letting the chaos enter us. It's freeing to realize that chaos comes at us, but it is not us. It's an external force trying to get in—and we have the power to deny entry. We can roll up the window.

My wife was naming how I became more chaotic during chaotic times. And the more things swirled, the worse I became.

What I really needed was hope. A hope not dependent on what was going on around me. A hope that was bigger than me. Bigger than circumstances. One that could withstand the storms of life. But nothing I tried worked.

What are we to do when we reach the end of ourselves and still don't have answers?

With God, we can enter the chaos
without letting the chaos enter us.
It's freeing to realize that chaos
comes at us, but it is not us.

Once chaos gets within us, it hardly
matters which direction it takes us.
It has us. And whether we show it
on the outside or not,
our internal world is in trouble.

When We Let It In

Regardless of how it begins, the initial impact of chaos is to make you more chaotic.

You become shut down. Or spun up.

You're easily offended. You complain and rant and grow irritated at everyone and everything. You demand others change for you but rarely consider ways you need to change for others. The impatience and anger grows until you no longer recognize yourself.

Or maybe you experience the opposite. You go numb to whatever happens. Shrug your shoulders and check out.

Once it gets within us, it hardly matters which direction it takes us. It has us. And whether we show it on the outside or not, our internal world is in trouble. The swirling chaos within affects our thoughts, our breathing, our heart rate, our ability to rest, sleep, or pay attention to others.

Regardless of how well you hide it, the result of chaos will always be *more* chaos.

To take this from abstract to real, I'll share a few personal ways I get taken out. These aren't overly dramatic life-or-death examples, but "any given Monday morning" moments.

Remember our definition of chaos:

Chaos is a destructive, fear-based force that prevents you from fully living. The ways it comes against you—large and small—are often intensely personal strikes meant to leave you empty.

It's important to note chaos comes against us in big and small ways. I'm guessing most parents who drives their kids to school can relate to this story I'm about to tell.

I like things to be calm. I like people to get along. Especially my kids. My three teenage kids.

Before any of them could drive, I'd take them to school each morning in my truck. Most days, at least two of the three would sleep through their alarms. So while I tried to get myself ready, I'd run back and forth to their rooms to make sure they were up and going. One morning went like this:

"Good morning," I said, flipping the lights on and off. Staying calm and kind.

"Stop it! Get out of my room!"

"We're leaving for school in ten minutes."

"I know! I'm awake!"

"You're in bed with your eyes closed."

"Then why didn't you wake me up earlier?"

"I'm not your alarm. And I did. Four times."

We raced downstairs, everyone in a crabby mood. I felt irritation trying to get in. My beautiful wife had made a hot breakfast that no one had time to eat. We grabbed a few slices of bacon and piled into the truck. But not before a disagreement on who would sit in the front passenger seat.

At this point, I could only make it to the school on time if there were no other vehicles on the road and I caught every green light. If we were late, the kids would get an unexcused tardy. I felt tension all around me.

An argument erupted over who got to pick the first song. Then about how long the song was. The others shouted louder to make their case. Then one of them cranked the volume up so high that the bass shook the coffee out of my cup.

The car ahead of me hit the brakes. An accident ahead was slowing traffic. My grandmother could have ridden a bike faster than we were moving. We weren't going to make it on time. No way.

I started to let the chaos in. "Turn the stereo down. And quit arguing."

The two in the back kept at it. One said something rude to the other. Then to me. The music somehow grew louder. We were so, so late.

And I let it in. The chaos of the morning, the traffic, the music, the arguments. It went from around me to within me.

Then two words I hate erupted from my mouth. "SHUT. UP."

My chaos was louder than the music or the argument. And it shut everyone and everything down. We rode the rest of the way in silence. No music. No talking. No laughter. Their eyes down. Their spirits crushed.

I like calm. But I didn't bring it. I brought a void.

I like getting along. But I didn't rescue the situation. I tanked it.

I hated myself for what I let in. And then for what came out of me.

The power of our words isn't a little thing.

> It only takes a spark, remember, to set off a forest fire. A careless or wrongly placed word out of your

> mouth can do that. By our speech we can ruin the world, turn harmony to chaos, throw mud on a reputation, send the whole world up in smoke and go up in smoke with it, smoke right from the pit of hell. (James 3:5–6 MSG)

The exhausting ride ended with us pulling up to the school ten minutes late. They got out without saying good-bye. I drove off feeling like a failure.

Chaos won that morning.

When We Don't Let It In

Did I mention I have teenagers?

Not every day involves the truck ride from hell. I don't always blow it.

In my better moments, I don't let chaos in. I had one recently.

My daughter had a really hard day. She wasn't in a good mood. I came downstairs while she and my wife were having one of those kitchen conversations that was heading toward a disagreement before escalating into an argument. I caught enough of the back-and-forth to know what the issue was. And I found the swirling chaos around them wanting to snag me as well.

I felt the urge to step in, interrupt the tension, and shut it down.

But this time, I didn't let the chaos in.

Instead, I took a deep breath and calmly invited my daughter to sit down in our family room.

She was unhappy about a situation. And unhappy to be talking to me about it.

Rather than be offended by her tone or words, I spoke love back to her. Doing so allowed me to bring beauty, life, and order into the place disorder had been minutes earlier.

She soon shared what was really going on at a heart level. It had little to do with the initial issue. I listened. I was comfortable with the silence and the messiness. As James 1:19 reminds us, "It is best to listen much, speak little, and not become angry"(TLB).

The turbulence ended with tenderness, tears, and a hug.

I like calm. I like people getting along. But rather than wait for those things to happen and be irritated when it doesn't, I ushered those things in.

Chaos lost that evening.

When we let chaos inside us,
our strengths can go toxic fast.

I started justifying my anger,
which is a dangerous action.
Because when we rationalize
these kinds of things, we're an
inch away from letting chaos in.

When Our Strength Fails Us

What are you particularly good at? What areas of your life do you navigate really well?

I'm good at making things happen. I'm quick to identify a problem and fix it, sure that whatever it is, I'll get to the bottom and come out on top. A good friend says I have tenacity. Which I like. It sounds a lot more positive than *relentless* or *driven*.

But when we let chaos inside us, our strengths can go toxic fast.

Like the morning when my wife and I were sharing a vehicle because our other car was in the shop. We had taken our kids to school and merged into the drop-off line. This is a single lane for parents to drive up and let their kids out. It flows fast because the whole point is to pull up, have your kids pop out, and move on.

After our kids got out, I started to leave, but the car in front of us had parked instead of pulling out. I was trapped in the line until she moved.

I could feel irritation trying to get in. I waited a few seconds. She appeared to be checking texts on her phone. Meanwhile, the line of vehicles behind us was piling up.

It's not that I had to be anywhere in the next few minutes. I had plenty of time. Yet I found myself irritated that she was holding everyone up in such a selfish or oblivious way.

Now offense tried to get in. It took everything in me not to lay on the horn or get out of my car and go knock on her windshield and motion her forward.

I glanced at my wife. She was fine. Totally at peace.

When I see a problem, I want to fix it. This parked car had turned into a world-class problem, and it was inconveniencing *me*. I started to wonder why the school didn't have a monitor to keep the cars moving. Clearly, their system was broken if any car at any moment could turn the drive-through into a parking lot. Where was the order?

Now I was angry with the woman and the school planning committee. Plus, I was starting to feel claustrophobic.

"It's okay, Allen." My wife gently patted my knee.

But I didn't feel okay.

My hand moved toward the horn. My truck has a really loud horn.

"Don't do it, Allen. Just be patient."

I felt trapped. I was irritated. I wanted to set this injustice right.

I started justifying my anger, which is a dangerous action. Because when we rationalize these kinds of things, we're an inch away from letting chaos in.

Only by the grace of God—and my wife's presence—I did nothing. Well, that's not true. I did nothing embarrassing. I found a way to slowly go back and forth until I could angle my truck around the woman's parked car.

That was years ago. I often wonder if she's still parked there.

In all seriousness, I know there's a really good part of me that can make things happen. I see problems and how they could be fixed. *This is a roadblock. This needs to move.*

But chaos can shift my strength to a weakness when I start to see *people* as the roadblock. My wife saw the woman in front of us as a mom who was likely overwhelmed or simply distracted. My wife was filled with empathy. I saw her as a problem to be overcome. And I was filled with irritation.

My strength, when harnessed, can bring order to disorder.

But that same strength, when I let outside pressures and toxins in, becomes a weakness.

Once we let chaos in, the only thing we can create . . . is more chaos.

While this voyage isn't the *Love Boat,* it also doesn't need to be the *Titanic.* Not if you understand what's really going on.

In This World

I found myself wondering why God didn't give us more advance warning about the chaos that was coming at us. I mean, if only he had, things would be so much better.

And then I realized, he did.

Jesus was upfront about this life. He tells us matter-of-factly:

> In this world, you will have trouble. (John 16:33 NIV)

The word he used for *trouble* could also mean "affliction," "pressure," or "harassment." And, I would suggest, "chaos." Jesus isn't just wanting us to be aware. He's wanting us to be prepared.

Think of it this way: You're on a ship and the captain suddenly announces, "We're about to hit an iceberg!" That's accurate information, but it's also void of hope. It's an observation that points to the likely demise of the ship and everyone on it. The words only create panic.

But if the captain instead said at the start of the voyage, "In this water, there will be icebergs," well, that's different. He's giving his passengers a heads-up to the dangers—and a hope. He's aware of trouble yet is also calm. You sense he knows how to navigate it.

Mythically speaking, we live in a sea filled with looming icebergs. Some are hidden below the surface of the dark, murky waters. Others protrude like mammoth frozen mountains, taunting any ship that enters its path.

We'd be fools to count on smooth sailing. Some of the icebergs out there will rock and shake our confidence. Our vessel is going to suffer some damage. It's just part of the journey. Anyone who says otherwise is either clueless or selling false assurances.

But while this voyage isn't the *Love Boat*, it also doesn't need to be the *Titanic*. Not if you understand what's really going on. Once you do, the icebergs no longer catch you off guard.

When Jesus says we'll have trouble in this world, he's not being negative. He's naming reality. There is chaos in this world. It's not a possibility. It's a certainty.

But his words reflect an even greater certainty. Let's look at his complete statement by including the sentences that bookend his warning of trouble:

> I have told you these things, so that in me you may have peace. In this world, you will have trouble. But take heart! I have overcome the world. (John 16:33 NIV)

First, he tells us his motive. He's come to give us peace.

The word he actually uses for *peace* signifies wholeness or completeness. And he says the way to such peace is "in me." We only find peace in and through him. Perhaps because everything (including you) was made through him (John 1:3).

But is it realistic to think that this foundation of peace can keep us safe in the midst of chaos?

Often, my pushback comes because I just want Jesus to clear away the chaos of my life. I view peace as the absence of chaos rather than something that is possible in the midst of chaos.

Jesus tells a fascinating parable that touches on this very issue.

> Anyone who listens to my teaching and follows it is wise, like a person who builds a house on solid rock. Though the rain comes in torrents and the floodwaters rise and the winds beat against that house, it won't collapse because it is built on bedrock. But anyone who hears my teaching and doesn't obey it is foolish, like a person who builds a house on sand. When the rains and floods come and the winds beat against that house, it will collapse with a mighty crash. (Matthew 7:24–27 NLT)

Both people encounter the same external chaos—torrents of rain, floodwaters, and winds blasting the homes. The outer storm comes at the houses with equal intensity. Yet one person's home survives because of its foundation.

The foundation isn't human wisdom. It is Jesus. He tells us that in this world we will have trouble. No one gets a pass from the swirling chaos around them. Yet Jesus comes to give us peace. Not peace dependent on a peaceful world. But peace in the middle of a shaken world.

That sounds great. But whatever I'm doing hasn't been working all that well. When storms hit, my peace decreases and fear increases. Am I missing something?

Jesus comes to give us peace. Not peace dependent on a peaceful world. But peace in the middle of a shaken world.

What's Been Overcome

I read the verse again and realize I have been overlooking the last two sentences:

> But take heart! I have overcome the world.
> (John 16:33 NIV)

I've been losing heart because I hadn't fully embraced his full victory over chaos.

He doesn't merely say he can handle the trouble of this world. He doesn't just promise to overcome the chaos. His next statement goes exponentially beyond that.

Jesus says we are to take heart because *he already has overcome the entire world.* It's the difference between a ship's captain saying, "In this sea are icebergs, but don't worry" and, "Don't worry, because I've already overcome this entire sea."

See the difference? One is bravado. One is proof.

You're drawn to the captain who says he's already overcome the sea. But you still have a few questions. You clear your throat. *Um, sir. Do you mean you've outmaneuvered an iceberg like this before? Or that you've made it through this part of the waterway with minimal loss?*

"No. I'm not talking about an iceberg or waterway." With a wink he smiles. "You're thinking way too small. I've completely overcome the entire sea."

Now that's a captain you'd follow anywhere. That's who Jesus is. If we stay with him, we no longer have to be shaken by the storms of life—whether outside us or within us.

Chaos wants us to surrender. Instead, we need to remember who our captain is.

He's not working up a sweat to get us through. He can handle whatever chaos comes our way. He's already overcome the entire world. And that's good. Because our goal isn't merely to survive the chaos, but to overcome it.

If your current approach to chaos isn't working, you'll find this journey immensely helpful. Even transformative. But fair warning—we don't overcome from a place of overconfidence. This journey only works if we enter into it humbly with God. If we admit our solo ways haven't worked.

In our own strength, we will lose to chaos every time. But when we face it with God, well, everything changes.

Jesus says we are to take heart
because he already has overcome
the entire world.
It's the difference between
a ship's captain saying, "In this
sea are icebergs, but don't worry"
and, "Don't worry, because I've
already overcome this entire sea."

Our goal isn't merely to survive
the chaos, but to overcome it.

The Anchor of Our Hope

Yes, in the sea there are icebergs. But when our captain is Jesus, we can take heart. He has seen everything. He has no fear of icebergs. He's overcome the entire sea. And because of that, we don't have to let fear of the icebergs freeze our hearts or sink our hopes. With his help, we can avoid many of the troubles at sea.

Still, some icebergs will hit hard where we're most vulnerable and when we least expect it. The reason this doesn't tank our hope is that our hope doesn't rest in the ship. Or upon a smooth sea.

Our hope is entirely in the captain. He is our anchor. No matter what happens, we remain with him. Because to him, we are far more than passengers. We are sons and daughters of God.

On this journey, you'll see it's possible to overcome the troubles that want to overwhelm you. No longer will external chaos make you chaotic internally. And you'll discover the power to transform the chaos into beauty, life, and order.

I want to give you some immediate encouragement. *God is for you* in the midst of your battles against chaos. Check out the psalmist's words about his active involvement and love for you at this very moment:

But me he caught—reached all the way
from sky to sea; he pulled me out
Of that ocean of hate, that enemy chaos,
the void in which I was drowning.
They hit me when I was down,
but God stuck by me.
He stood me up on a wide-open field;
I stood there saved—surprised to be loved!
(Psalm 18:16–19 MSG)

Imagine being free of chaos for just one day. Think of how much lighter you would feel. How much better you would rest. How much calmer you would be.

That would be the best day of your life. Not because the world is suddenly void of chaos, but because you are.

Now, what if that one day could happen every day?

That's the destination we're sailing to in this book. Right in the middle of a sea filled with icebergs.

When we start with God,
he gives us wisdom.
But he also gives us something
far more valuable: himself.

If the Creator of everything offered
you absolutely anything,
what would you ask for . . . really?

In Need of a Sage

I tend to call out to God only after I'm exhausted from trying to navigate my own icebergs. Not a smart strategy. Kind of like driving through the car wash with my window down.

I'm learning anew the value of asking for God's wisdom on the front end.

> Wisdom begins with respect for the Lord,
> and understanding begins with knowing the
> Holy One. (Proverbs 9:10 NCV)

But it's not just wisdom we're after. It's the joy of doing life with God.

> Take delight in the Lord,
> and he will give you the desires of your heart.
> (Psalm 37:4 NIV)

When we start with God, he gives us wisdom. But he also gives us something far more valuable: himself. That's why he is the only one worthy to be the sage in our journey.

When it came to chaos, I sensed more was at play than what I could see, but I was at a loss for answers. So I asked God to lead me on a journey of wisdom.

My quest reminded me of King Solomon's story. He was the wisest man who ever lived. That part didn't remind me of me. But his hunger to learn did. You may recall Solomon was David's son. What I'd forgotten was how he gained his wisdom. As the story goes, God offered him anything.

Stop there. If the Creator of everything offered you absolutely anything, what would you ask for . . . really?

God made that astonishing offer to Solomon. But God also made Solomon. He didn't just know the man inside out. He infused certain desires into Solomon before he was born.

Imagine Solomon pondering his options as God holds the pre-selected perfect gift behind his back, excited to give Solomon his heart's desire.

Yes, he asked Solomon what he wanted. But I wonder if he was also saying, "Solomon, I know you better than anyone. I can give you anything. Ask what I want to give you!"

In a sense, that's what Solomon did. He asked the Creator of his heart what his heart most longed for. He asked for wisdom and knowledge.

God was delighted—but not surprised.

> God, the Master, was delighted with Solomon's response. And God said to him, "Because you have asked for this and haven't grasped after a long life, or riches, or the doom of your enemies, but you have asked for the ability to lead and govern well, I'll give you what you've asked for—I'm giving you a wise and mature heart. There's never been one like you before; and there'll be no one after." (1 Kings 3:10–12 MSG)

Do you see the incredible interplay between God and Solomon? We are sons and daughters of the same wildly generous God. He stands ready to grant us our heart's desire and wisdom beyond imagination.

But there is a condition.

When the Creator of stars, stallions,
and sunsets offers to reveal
marvelous, great, unsearchable,
and remarkable things,
this generosity should set
our hearts racing.

The Offer of Wisdom

God's offer to grant wisdom beyond our own understanding appears to be based on our desire to pursue life with him.

Here's how Scripture describes the process:

> Call to me and I will answer you. I'll tell you marvelous and wondrous things that you could never figure out on your own. (Jeremiah 33:3 MSG)

When we call out to God, he answers. That alone is astonishing.

But it gets even better. Did you catch what comes after that? God will then reveal "unsearchable things" (NIV) and "remarkable secrets you do not know about things to come" (NLT).

The invitation is to have our minds blown. To learn great and mighty things we do not know. To experience marvelous and wonderful insights we could never figure out on our own. To discover remarkable secrets of things yet to come.

Imagine how those things would enhance every aspect of your life.

But there's a condition.

It's promised only *if* we include God in the process.

No matter how wise or creative we may be, we'll never attain these kinds of insights on our own. They're only available through—and *with*—God.

When the Creator of stars, stallions, and sunsets offers to reveal marvelous, great, unsearchable, and remarkable things, this generosity should set our hearts racing. Our human limits no longer matter. The previously impossible is more than possible with God.

> For with God nothing will be impossible.
> (Luke 1:37 NKJV)

Jesus also reminds us that as we pursue life with him, he will reveal things that he has set in motion for us but tucked away since creation. Why? They are waiting until we are ready to discover them. Until we can be trusted with them.

> I will bring out into the open things hidden since the world's first day. (Matthew 13:35 MSG)

So I asked God for wisdom in this journey of overcoming chaos. My motive was immediate and personal. I was desperate to not lose heart in a time of growing chaos.

God not only met but exceeded my expectations.

I encourage you to ask God for wisdom on whatever is overwhelming you. Then expect his wisdom to permeate and inform everything you read here, or anywhere else, on this topic.

First Learn Stand. Then Learn Fly.

In the 1984 movie *The Karate Kid,* there is a famous scene where Mr. Miyagi is teaching his impatient student Daniel an essential truth: "First learn stand. Then learn fly. Nature's rule, Daniel-san, not mine."

There is a progression to what we're learning here.

First is standing, which is not letting chaos in. I'll address the learning to fly part soon, but we must master the first before considering the second.

So how do we not let chaos in? These five practices are a good start.

1. Stop allowing chaos to surprise you. Remember, Jesus said that in this world we'll have trouble. But because he has overcome it, we can take heart and have peace (John 16:33). So the first step is to be aware and have a game plan for what you'll do when it hits. This alone moves you from playing defense to offense.

2. Reject the lie. Acknowledge that a situation or person is chaotic and trying to make you fearful, but remember that giving in to chaos and fear is your choice. Chaos cannot invade your domain—your heart and your head—without

your permission. It wants you to believe you have no choice but to become chaotic when chaos hits. That's a lie. Remember the truth: Jesus has already overcome the whole world.

3. Guard your heart. When we turn to God, he gives us a new heart:

> I will give you one heart and a new spirit; I will take from you your hearts of stone and give you tender hearts of love for God, so that you can obey my laws and be my people, and I will be your God. (Ezekiel 11:19–20 TLB)

You have a new heart. Now the goal is to protect it from all that wants to come against it. Scripture puts it this way:

> Guard your heart above all else,
> for it determines the course of your life.
> (Proverbs 4:23 NLT)

Your heart is what the enemy is most after. And he will throw as much chaos at you at possible to cause you to lose heart or give it to the wrong things. That is why we must guard it.

4. Fill your heart with what's good. This isn't something to begin doing when chaos strikes. It's something to pursue daily, not reactively but proactively.

God offers to fill our hearts with things that bring us life, but again, we choose what goes in. If we choose to let chaos in, we become empty and void. If we fill ourselves with what God offers, we brim with life. If you find yourself responding to the storms of life in ways that aren't helpful, perhaps it's because you're filling yourself with the wrong substance.

So what should we fill our hearts with? In Deuteronomy 6:5–7, we're told:

> Love God, your God, with your whole heart: love him with all that's in you, love him with all you've got!
>
> Write these commandments that I've given you today on your hearts. Get them inside of you and then get them inside your children. Talk about them wherever you are, sitting at home or walking in the street; talk about them from the time you get up in the morning to when you fall into bed at night. (MSG)

It gets even better. Because the Holy Spirit actually resides in the hearts of all who love God, the perimeter of our hearts is defended by the Spirit. The fruit (or attributes) of the Holy Spirit provide us with nine layers of protection against the chaos trying to get in: love, joy, peace, patience, kindness, goodness, faithfulness, gentleness, and self-control (Galatians 5:22–23).

The Spirit infuses us with these internal gifts to help us keep fear, doubt, and all the rotten fruits of chaos out. If you feel chaos keeps finding a way in, ask the Holy Spirit for help. Perhaps you lack peace or kindness. Maybe you could use an infusion of self-control or patience. Rather than continue to try to fight outside rage with inner rage, watch what happens when you counter it with gentleness.

5. Let what's in flow out. When our hearts are filled with the fruit of the spirit, there won't be room for chaos to come in. Then we can respond to what comes against us by drawing upon the good within us. This way of living is transformative, and it's how we will eventually learn to fly.

These five steps are our first line of defense in this shaken world.

Chaos cannot invade your domain—your heart and your head—without your permission. It wants you to believe you have no choice but to become chaotic when chaos hits. That's a lie.

Your heart is what the enemy is
most after. And he will throw as
much chaos at you at possible
to cause you to lose heart or
give it to the wrong things.

What's at Stake?

Everything.

I'm not exaggerating. The goal of chaos is not just to mess with your to-do list or disrupt your day.

The goal of chaos is to destroy you.

Like a strategic chess game, the first moves matter. As we've seen, the opening move for chaos is to try to make us more chaotic. This occurs in a variety of large and small ways each day. We come home to a flooded basement. We get into our minivan and the kids are screaming. We open the overdue bill. The numbers on our cancer tests are going the wrong way.

We feel the chaos, swirling with fear, trying to rush in. Every time, it seeks to make us "less" us and "more" it. But what exactly does it gain by doing this?

In the wild, wolves seek to disorient their prey. They do this by waiting until nightfall. Then the beasts circle their target and begin their chilling howls. They create an illusion of hundreds of wolves. In reality there may be six or seven, spread out strategically. The goal is to convince their prey that they are legion.

The safest thing for the hunted animals to do would be to stay together. But they panic. They run. And they are devoured.

As are we when we allow chaos to have its way with us. It wants us to feel surrounded. Helpless. Hopeless. Because that's when we panic and lose our bearings.

Ultimately, we surrender our identity as sons and daughters of God.

That's why the right interpretation of what's really going on is so crucial. Though chaos wants us to fear the beast on the island, we don't have to give way to the wolves, no matter how loud they howl.

The Right Interpretation

The right interpretation changes everything.

When our children were young, we often had more month than money. The kids didn't fully understand, but they could sense when times were tight.

One night, I was reading to one of my sons in my bed. At the end of the story, he looked at me and said, "Daddy, I'm sorry there's not much money." I smiled and assured him all was okay.

"But, Dad, I know it's tough."

"Why do you say that?"

"Well, I have my own bed. And so do my brother and sister."

"Right," I said.

"But you and mommy have to share a bed. Maybe one day when there's more money, you can each have your own bed."

I love that story. His heart was right but, well, his interpretation of what he saw was wrong.

Some people see a puzzle as a jumbled box of chaos. It's really a box of expertly created order separated into five hundred pieces. We're invited to bring order to it. But we have to see past the mess of pieces—to the larger image—to do so.

What if part of our destiny is to bring order to disorder?

Order is without question harder to bring into existence than disorder. Anyone can demolish what is. But destroyers rarely have blueprints for rebuilding something of beauty and order.

And let's not mistake order for control. There's an ocean of difference between the two. In fact, let's use the ocean as an example.

When God creates a body of water, the ocean is the result.

> Who else has held the oceans in his hand?
> Who has measured off the heavens with his fingers?
> (Isaiah 40:12 NLT)

The ocean is wild and untamed. It is beyond our control . . . but full of life. When humans try to create a body of water, we get a swimming pool. It is temperature controlled, depth controlled, chlorine controlled, and filter controlled. It is totally controlled, and it has no life.

Pursuing order is a creative act that restores things back to God's original intention. It brings freedom and life to something that has become disordered and no longer the truest form of what it was meant to be.

Motive matters here. We must be more expectant for what God is up to than making sure our expectations are achieved. That is what bringing order from disorder looks like. And it begins with accurately interpreting what is really going on, what's gone wrong, and why it can seem so personal.

Some people see a puzzle as a
jumbled box of chaos. It's really
a box of expertly created order
separated into five hundred pieces.
We're invited to bring order to it.

Order is without question harder to bring into existence than disorder. Anyone can demolish what is. But destroyers rarely have blueprints for rebuilding something of beauty and order.

Why Does It Seem Personal?

How many times has someone made a decision that impacts you in immensely personal ways and then glibly said, "Nothing personal"?

Their disclaimer doesn't change the fact that the decision is, in fact, personal.

We often view chaos as an impersonal force that plays out with the same generic implications for anyone in its path. Natural disasters, recessions, and viruses impact millions at once. And these things certainly have an impact on you.

But chaos has a personal aspect to it as well. Despite some opinions that chaos is random and couldn't possibly be designed to push our buttons or sabotage us, I couldn't disagree more. That just doesn't line up with real-life experiences.

Chaos comes against us like strategic personal strikes designed to take us out. What—or who—would want to do that?

Scripture tells us that our enemy is Satan, and he is a thief. What is he after?

> The thief's purpose is to steal, kill and destroy.
> My purpose is to give life in all its fullness.
> (John 10:10 TLB)

The enemy uses chaos as a customized force, or weapon, that is specifically designed to take us out in the places we are most vulnerable. And Jesus counters that, offering to fill us with life instead.

That's why so much of the chaos in your world seems personal. Because it is.

Pursuing order is a creative act that restores things back to God's original intention.

Perhaps that's why, like with
the fisherman on the shore,
Jesus simply asks us to follow him.
He doesn't first sit us down
and answer our every question.
Instead, he invites us into
the journey: *Follow me.*
Learn along the way.
Seek me more than answers.

Entering Uncharted Terrain

We are about to enter a far more treacherous part of the journey.

Before we do, it's important to pause and consider how far we've come. I feel energized and hope you do as well.

We are gaining clarity. We are several steps closer to unmasking chaos and revealing what it really is. Not from some hyperfascination with it, but from a desire to overcome and be free of it. To live chaos-free.

From what we've explored so far, it's clear that in this world we'll have trouble. That our past responses have been inadequate. And that we don't have to let it in. That's a good start.

But there is an unseen reality at play as well. One that might further explain why the chaos seems to take aim at us in such personal ways. And where God is in the midst of it all.

We must now make our way through enemy territory. Doing so is necessary to understand the likely origin of chaos. It is a topic the enemy would prefer you not know about. Because once you do, his attempts to take you out with chaos will be far less effective. His story, failures, and tactics will be exposed.

As we prepare to undertake this next part of our quest, it is crucial we stay close to God and resist the enemy. It's a good time to remember this council from Jesus' half-brother James:

> Therefore submit to God. Resist the devil and he will flee from you. (James 4:7 NKJV)

Jesus himself actively applied this strategy throughout his life. We see an especially powerful example when he traveled into the wilderness for forty days knowing the enemy would try and take him out. Though the enemy did his best to tempt him, Jesus didn't play his game. He didn't enter into a lengthy debate, question God, or become more chaotic. He simply responded with Scripture no matter what strategy the enemy threw at him. And after three failed attempts, the enemy fled (Matthew 4:1-11).

Submit to God and resist the enemy. That remains the only true path to transformation. As we'll see, it's a narrow path filled with challenges. But that's okay. Easy and best are rarely on the same path.

At this point in the journey, you likely have more questions than answers. I still do. But if we refuse to go further until all our upfront questions are answered, we'll forever remain right where we are. Still without answers and stubbornly stuck in the unknown.

Perhaps that's why, like with the fisherman on the shore, Jesus simply asks us to follow him. He doesn't first sit us down and answer our every question. Instead, he invites us into the journey: *Follow me. Learn along the way. Seek me more than answers.*

We know what chaos looks like in our lives. We've learned we don't have to let chaos in.

But what exactly is this substance that wants in? And why does it come against us in such personal ways? Especially, as we'll see, against our hearts and our creativity?

Take a deep breath. We're about to enter uncharted terrain as we explore the origin of chaos.

If we refuse to go further until
all our upfront questions are
answered, we'll forever remain
right where we are.
Still without answers and
stubbornly stuck in the unknown.

3

CHAOS

What God has given you
to do is beyond you, for you,
and never up to you.

A Second, Deeper Definition

What is chaos . . . really?

If chaos is what we want to overcome, then we must answer this basic question.

Not "What is its effect on us?" We're well aware of that.

But bigger questions. Origin questions. "Where did it come from?" "What is it a manifestation of?"

Curiosity compelled me to further my understanding of chaos. If I wanted to truly overcome it I had to know more.

You'll recall the Dictionary.com definition of chaos we encountered was both accurate and not particularly helpful. It could have applied to my confusion during high school math class.

A state of utter confusion or disorder.

It describes what's going on but not how to get out of it. Which, okay, isn't really the dictionary's job. But still. There had to be more.

I offered my own definition, which we'll use throughout this journey. But I also wondered if Dictionary.com had anything further to offer. So I returned to it and found a second definition that goes a little deeper. This one offers more than just a description of what chaos does. It hints at its origin:

The infinity of space or formless matter supposed to have preceded the existence of the ordered universe.

Okay. This feels deeper. It's certainly more mythic than the first definition.

Before the existence of our ordered universe, some substance or matter was already there that represented disorder. It was formless, empty, and void.

This definition of chaos touches on its ancient roots. But it's a mouthful. Reading it makes me feel like I've stepped into the middle of a Stephen Hawking lecture. The words sound important and heavy, but what is it saying?

And how in the world does this definition relate to screaming kids in the car or losing a home to a fire?

A Hidden Underlying Cause

As I continued my research, I came across numerous references to chaos spanning movies, literature, and science.

John Milton, in his epic 1667 poem *Paradise Lost*, imagines what could have happened in the times leading up to and during the tragic fall in Eden. In it, he personifies Chaos, describing the entity as "eternal anarchy" (II, 896), "wild abyss" (II, 917), and "the hollow dark" (II, 953).

I also came across the term *chaos theory*. I vaguely remember it from high school science class. Or maybe it was something Ian Malcolm said in one of the *Jurassic Park* movies.

According to Britannica.com:

> Chaos theory, in mechanics and mathematics, [is] the study of apparently random or unpredictable behaviour in systems governed by deterministic laws. A more accurate term, *deterministic chaos*, suggests a paradox because it connects two notions that are familiar and commonly regarded as incompatible. The first is that of randomness or unpredictability . . . . The second notion is that of deterministic motion. (March 2020).

Chaos theory attempts to explain complex systems that appear to behave in seemingly random manners—yet really aren't acting randomly because they demonstrate "deterministic motion." In other words, something more is going on. There is purpose or intent within the chaos.

The sense is that it is only *apparently* random because an underlying cause is at play, though it is difficult to see.

An underlying cause.

That seems to indicate purpose . . . or intent.

Could it be possible there's an ancient yet hidden underlying cause to the chaos in our lives? If so, then it's not simply random resistance we face. At least not most of the time. It is customized chaos designed to work against us.

It was time to upgrade my search.

But if chaos existed before time, how was I supposed to research that?

Thankfully, the sage on our journey is the Creator of time.

Let's look at chaos from his perspective.

Could it be possible there's an
ancient yet hidden underlying
cause to the chaos in our lives?
If so, then it's not simply
random resistance we face.

Chaos is primal.

But it isn't eternal.

It didn't always exist.

Beginnings

God, Jesus, and the Holy Spirit are eternal.

Everything else has a beginning. Including us. Our universe. And chaos.

It can sure seem like chaos has been around forever. It ravages the earth this very second, yet certainly isn't new. It's been around since long before we were born. Our parents, grandparents, great grandparents all faced it. The ancients wrote about it.

Yet it hasn't always been around.

Chaos is primal. But it isn't eternal. It didn't always exist.

So when did it start?

A drowning man doesn't
consider the origin of water
as he's gasping for air.

First Appearance

When did chaos first appear?

That's a huge question. It feels significant. But it's not one I think to ask in the middle of a turbulent situation. A drowning man doesn't consider the origin of water as he's gasping for air.

In this part of the journey, we're contending for clarity.

When did chaos begin?

While we can't be absolutely sure, God does provide us with some clues.

Most from a Judeo-Christian background would say the instigating event was when Adam and Eve, in the middle of paradise, chose the serpent's way over God's order. You can read about that tragic downfall in Genesis 3. It was unquestionably a massive, world-altering shakeup. Scripture says that's when sin and death entered our world.

But not chaos.

It was already present in our universe. After all, wouldn't the one who tempted Adam and Eve toward chaos already be filled with it?

If it predates the fall in Eden, when do we see an earlier appearance? There are only so many sentences in Genesis before we get to the story of Adam and Eve, so our search shouldn't take long.

Perhaps it was brought into existence during the days of creation? But no, chaos is already present in

Genesis 1:2. Did chaos begin before the "in the beginning" of Genesis 1:1?

Hang on. Things are about to accelerate.

Darkness Over the Deep

One of the most intriguing passages in the entire Bible makes its appearance early, in the second verse of the first book.

Genesis 1:2.

It's a verse most people skim because it is confusing. At first read, it does appear to be a diversion from the creation story. So let's start with the familiar, Genesis 1:1:

> In the beginning God created the heavens and the earth. (NIV)

It seems like this should come next:

> And God said, "Let there be light," and there was light. (NIV)

But that's Genesis 1:3. There's something that happens between these two verses. Something epic, mysterious, and wild.

> Now the earth was formless and empty, darkness was over the surface of the deep, and the Spirit of God was hovering over the waters.
> (Genesis 1:2 NIV)

Whatever's going on here seems an abrupt shift from the Bible's opening words. Genesis starts by introducing us to God as Creator. But then, in the very next verse, it's like we jump to an entirely different story of his Spirit brooding over a formless, empty, dark, watery substance.

What image comes to mind when you read this verse? If you were a making a movie, where and how would this scene play out? If you were a painter, how would you capture it on canvas? Not thematically but literally. Because it literally happened. What did it look like?

I'm intrigued at how Eugene Peterson describes this moment in *The Message*:

> Earth was a soup of nothingness, a bottomless emptiness, an inky blackness. God's Spirit brooded like a bird above the watery abyss.
> (Genesis 1:2 MSG)

God's Spirit is compared to a brooding bird. *Brooded* is a word we don't hear much, but it refers to a bird spreading its wings to protect or nurture. It signifies a live-giving act taking place over a "bottomless emptiness."

What exactly is going on here?

Tohu VaVohu

Though even theologians don't fully agree on what is happening in Genesis 1:2, most would say whatever else is at play, this watery, murky substance is being transformed from disorder into order.

The phrase that conveys this thought in Hebrew is *Tohu VaVohu*. Although this isn't a term we hear much today, these words offer much light on what is happening.

We'll look at each word separately, then put them together. The *Va* in *VaVohu* means "and," so the two key words are *Tohu* and *Vohu*.

Tohu means "formless and unshaped." The unformed needs to be formed.

Vohu means "void and empty." The unfilled waits to be filled.

The words *formlessness*, *confusion*, *unreality*, *emptiness*, *futility*, *meaninglessness*, *nothing*, and *waste* all seem to be represented by this mystical-sounding phrase.

Tohu VaVohu only shows up a few other times in Scripture. When it does, it's as a reference to an unmaking of what was made or a return to a state of chaos, such as the prophet Jeremiah describes here:

> I looked at the earth—
> it was back to pre-Genesis chaos and emptiness.
> I looked at the skies,
> and not a star to be seen. (Jeremiah 4:23 MSG)

But let's look at the first use of this phrase here in Genesis. What is God's response to this chaotic state of disorder?

Creation.

In Genesis 1:2, his Spirit broods over the empty chaos. The sense is that the Spirit has a calm assurance above the swirling chaos. There is no contest here. The Spirit's presence is peaceful yet powerful and assured.

God chooses this unshaped, swirling void to be his canvas. Before him is nothingness and disorder. Not the environment most of us would want to create in—or create from. Yet God is not deterred. He doesn't wait for the chaos to leave before beginning. Whether it was a void of nothingness or primeval watery chaos, the Creator, in this most daring, brilliant act of blazing beauty, illuminates and ignites it with light and life and order.

In the act of creation, God's canvas wasn't a beautiful, peaceful studio. It was chaotic murkiness.

God speaks light (Genesis 1:3) and initiates shaping and filling the Tohu VaVohu through a process known as the days of creation.

We'll look at the creation process in the next section. It's full of wonder and awe.

Long after writing "The Last Snow Globe," I discovered something fascinating about the phrase Tohu VaVohu. It can also be translated as "to be astonished." But the astonishment being described is at how the chaos is astonishingly empty. The focus is misplaced. Yes, we are to be astonished—but not at the beast on island. Instead, we are to be astonished at God and his endless goodness.

For now, it's essential to understand that God's objective wasn't simply to observe chaos. He wasn't a meteorologist reporting the weather. God, through his presence and power, was focused on changing the chaos. And he did.

Yet we still haven't arrived at the origin of chaos. In Genesis 1:2, it was already there—wherever "there" was.

But how do we continue our search if chaos predates Genesis?

Yes, we are to be astonished—
but not at the beast on island.
Instead, we are to be astonished
at God and his endless goodness.

A Toxic Choice

Before our world began—before time began—another story was well underway.

Remember, God has always existed. He is the eternal Creator. He didn't start creating with our world, hoping things would work out. Creativity is part of his essence.

Before he made the earth, God created the angelic beings. In the passage below, angels are shouting praise during the creation of earth.

> Where were you when I created the earth?
> Tell me, since you know so much!
> Who decided on its size? Certainly you'll know that!
> Who came up with the blueprints and measurements?
> How was its foundation poured,
> and who set the cornerstone,
> While the morning stars sang in chorus
> and all the angels shouted praise?
> (Job 38: 4–7 MSG)

These angelic beings live in the presence of God. And their numbers are immense.

> A river of fire was flowing,
> coming out from before him.
> Thousands upon thousands attended him;
> ten thousand times ten thousand stood before him. (Daniel 7:10 NIV)

> Then I looked and heard the voice of many angels, numbering thousands upon thousands, and ten thousand times ten thousand. (Revelation 5:11 NIV)

God also made other creatures. In Ezekiel 1, we see four that are distinct from the angels.

> The four creatures looked like a blazing fire, or like fiery torches. Tongues of fire shot back and forth between the creatures, and out of the fire, bolts of lightning. The creatures flashed back and forth like strikes of lightning . . .
>
> Over the heads of the living creatures was something like a dome, shimmering like a sky full of cut glass, vaulted over their heads. Under the dome one set of wings was extended toward the others, with another set of wings covering their bodies. When they moved I heard their wings—it was like the roar of a great waterfall, like the voice of The Strong God, like the noise of a battlefield. When they stopped, they folded their wings.
>
> And then, as they stood with folded wings, there was a voice from above the dome over their heads. Above the dome there was something that looked like a throne, sky-blue like a sapphire, with a humanlike figure towering above the throne. From what I could see, from the waist up he looked like burnished bronze and from the waist down like a blazing fire. Brightness everywhere!

> The way a rainbow springs out of the sky on a rainy day—that's what it was like. It turned out to be the Glory of God! (1:13-14, 22–28 MSG)

When we consider the realm of angelic and spiritual beings, it's clear that God's creativity was vast and diverse.

At some point, one of the angels, a created being named Lucifer, decided he no longer wanted to worship the Creator. He sought to be the one in charge. A created being demanded to rise above the one who gave him life. He rejected a supporting role. He wanted the story to be about him.

Maybe his offense was in how God elevated Jesus above every created being, "far higher than any angel in rank and rule" as stated below.

> After he finished the sacrifice for sins, the Son took his honored place high in the heavens right alongside God, far higher than any angel in rank and rule. Did God ever say to an angel, "You're my Son; today I celebrate you" or "I'm his Father, he's my Son"? When he presents his honored Son to the world, he says, "All angels must worship him." (Hebrews 1:3–6 MSG)

Whether due to this or something else, we see how his ego ultimately darkened his heart:

> You said in your heart,
> "I will ascend to the heavens;
> I will raise my throne
> above the stars of God." (Isaiah 14:13 NIV)

Don't miss where the spark first began: in his heart. Over time, the seeds of doubt grew in intensity. Rage, offense, and fury fueled a desire to overtake God. Could the empty void Lucifer allowed to grow in his heart—that vile mix of emotions and fear and hate—be the birth of chaos?

It amazes me how the heart is central to everything. How might things be different in our world today had Lucifer guarded his heart? As far as we know, this is the first time a created being chose life without God. But it was even more severe than that. He wanted to completely overtake God.

Scripture makes it clear that Lucifer, or Satan, is our enemy (1 Peter 5:8), accuser (Revelation 12:10), and tempter. He even unsuccessfully tried to tempt Jesus in the wilderness (Matthew 4:1–11).

Yet Lucifer himself had no tempter. He freely made his toxic choice in the presence of a perfect God in an unfallen environment.

> For God cannot be tempted by evil, nor does He Himself tempt anyone. (James 1:13 NKJV)

Does God give us any additional detail on the enemy's downfall?

Yes. Quite a bit.

Once a Guardian Cherub

There's a fascinating passage in Ezekiel that documents the fall of the king of Tyre. Yet many scholars also believe these words refer to an earlier, even more toxic downfall. The fall of Lucifer.

The descriptions below are beyond the capacity of any human. Here's how Ezekiel puts it:

> You were the seal of perfection,
> full of wisdom and perfect in beauty.
> You were in Eden,
> the garden of God;
> every precious stone adorned you:
> carnelian, chrysolite and emerald,
> topaz, onyx and jasper,
> lapis lazuli, turquoise and beryl.
> Your settings and mountings were made of gold;
> on the day you were created they were prepared.
> You were anointed as a guardian cherub,
> for so I ordained you.
> You were on the holy mount of God;
> you walked among the fiery stones.
> You were blameless in your ways
> from the day you were created
> till wickedness was found in you.

Through your widespread trade
you were filled with violence,
and you sinned.
So I drove you in disgrace from the mount of God,
and I expelled you, guardian cherub,
from among the fiery stones.
Your heart became proud
on account of your beauty,
and you corrupted your wisdom
because of your splendor.
So I threw you to the earth;
I made a spectacle of you before kings.
(Ezekiel 28:12–17 NIV)

Notice he was created blameless but wickedness was found in him. Why? Because his heart became proud and corrupted his wisdom. Violence filled him. And the chaos he birthed within then flowed out.

We get another glimpse of Lucifer when Isaiah declares the downfall of the king of Babylon. Again the focus seems to shift to an entity far more evil and powerful than even this depraved man.

We looked at a portion of this verse in the last chapter. Now we'll examine it more fully.

How you have fallen from heaven,
morning star, son of the dawn!
You have been cast down to the earth,
you who once laid low the nations!
You said in your heart,
"I will ascend to the heavens;
I will raise my throne

above the stars of God;
I will sit enthroned on the mount of assembly,
on the utmost heights of Mount Zaphon
I will ascend above the tops of the clouds;
I will make myself like the Most High."
But you are brought down to the realm of the dead,
to the depths of the pit. (Isaiah 14:12–15 NIV)

I believe these surreal images give us a glimpse into the fall of the enemy.

But Lucifer wasn't content to go down alone.

Imagine the arrogance.
Created beings trying to
overtake their Creator.

The Rebellion in Heaven

We don't know how long Lucifer nurtured the chaos within him, but ultimately it spilled out, just as it has for all who have allowed it into their hearts throughout history.

The internal chaos birthed in Lucifer's heart spread to other angelic beings. He may have begun by stirring doubt. Remember, these beings are in God's presence. They don't require faith to believe in God. He's right there. They are with God face-to-face. It's mind-blowing so many of these angels rebelled against God. They chose Lucifer, a created angelic being just like them, over their Creator.

As hard as it is to fathom, Scripture suggests he convinced one of every three angels to turn against their Creator.

> Then another sign appeared in heaven: an enormous red dragon with seven heads and ten horns and seven crowns on its heads. Its tail swept a third of the stars out of the sky and flung them to the earth. (Revelation 12:3 NIV)

This ultimately led to a rebellion against the Creator of heaven . . . and against order. It was an attempted *coup d'état* aimed at overthrowing God. Imagine the arrogance. Created beings trying to overtake their Creator. Yet surely these corrupted angels whispered and plotted and strategized in the hopes they would be successful. And finally they struck.

We don't have the exact scriptural account for that battle, but this passage from Revelation gives us a very close glimpse into the spiritual war of Heaven, either recounting the original battle, or one that comes after, though much like it:

> Then war broke out in heaven. Michael and his angels fought against the dragon, and the dragon and his angels fought back. But he was not strong enough, and they lost their place in heaven. The great dragon was hurled down—that ancient serpent called the devil, or Satan, who leads the whole world astray. He was hurled to the earth, and his angels with him. (Revelation 12:7–9 NIV)

But this battle isn't his only one. We'll now look what happens when he turns his focus to Adam and Eve.

The Rebellion on Earth

In the first rebellion, the enemy chose life without God. He's been trying to get the rest of creation to make the same choice ever since.

The enemy continued his toxic strategy with a new audience. This time he appeared in a new form—as a serpent—but used the same tactic he did with the angels. He hoped to turn their hearts in the same way: By infusing doubt about God's goodness. By bringing his chaotic presence into Eden.

I'm fascinated by how Tim Mackie and Jon Collins, cofounders of BibleProject, describe what's going on in their video titled *The Satan & Demons*:

> In Genesis 3, we meet a creature who's in a state of rebellion against his Creator. . . . It distorts what God has purposed for good, ruining and dragging creation back into darkness and disorder. So these humans join the spiritual rebel, which leads them back into chaos and death.

On BibleProject's website, an article titled "Chaos Monster" by Andy Patton accompanies this video and offers this intriguing insight:

What do we know about this serpent? First, he is bad news. This is a creature who is on a mission to disrupt God's good, ordered world—a chaos monster. The serpent is the Bible's first portrayal of evil and independence from God. From this point on, when the authors want to talk about evil, they use serpent and dragon imagery. Second, the serpent's own chaos-mission isn't enough; he also tries to persuade others to join. The first humans take the bait, and a pattern is established: spiritual rebellion behind human rebellion; spiritual powers behind earthly evil.

Yet Adam and Eve had a choice.

Like the angels, they had experienced God's presence firsthand. For instance, God discusses the trees of the garden with Adam, including which one to avoid (Genesis 2:16-17). He brings the animals before Adam and has him creatively name them (Genesis 2:19).

And God knows the desires of our heart (Psalm 37:4), even desires we can't fully articulate because they have never been brought to life yet. That's what happens when God says it isn't good for Adam to be without a female companion (Genesis 2:18). He knows what Adam desires before Adam does. And Scripture reveals that God walked in the garden in the cool of the day (Genesis 3:8).

Did their encounters with God last for just a few days or for years prior to the fall? We don't know. But we do know this: they knew God.

And, like the fallen angels, Adam and Eve tragically chose to rebel by following a created being rather than the Creator.

The enemy also wanted to be the hero of the story. He risked everything to force that to happen. But he simply went from being a supporting character for good to the antagonist and scorn of the universe.

He chose the wrong story and has been trying to get humans to do the same ever since.

How could anyone's creativity not
suffer a catastrophic loss
when it comes totally
untethered from the Creator?

The Enemy of Creation

When Lucifer made the choice to move against God, he didn't just become the enemy of the Creator, he became the enemy of creation.

Perhaps that's why creation is still groaning.

> For all creation is waiting eagerly for that future day when God will reveal who his children really are. Against its will, all creation was subjected to God's curse. But with eager hope, the creation looks forward to the day when it will join God's children in glorious freedom from death and decay. For we know that all creation has been groaning as in the pains of childbirth right up to the present time. (Romans 8:19–22 NLT)

When he tried to elevate himself above all, he revolted against everything that had been created by God. The created being Lucifer forfeited his place in heaven as he chose self over God. War over worship. Hate over humility.

He lost all intimacy and fellowship with God. And, because he lost his connection to the Creator, I believe he also lost his ability to create. How could anyone's creativity not suffer a catastrophic loss when it comes totally untethered from the Creator?

Knowingly or not, he exchanged creativity for chaos. Through it, he brings disorder, destruction, disruption and death wherever he goes. But he cannot create out of nothing. Only God can do that. And he cannot create anything eternal. Only God and those who create with him can do that. The best he can do is move against who God is. He has nothing new to offer. He only tries to counter what is true and good. He is reactionary. He is predictable. And ultimately he is empty and void.

Agents of Chaos

Scripture is clear on the three core objectives of the enemy:

> The thief comes only to steal and kill and destroy (John 10:10 NIV)

He wants to steal our hopes and talents, kill us or numb our hearts, and destroy our dreams and faith. Union with our Creator is the enemy's ultimate target.

He wanted to steal God's place as Creator. He was willing to kill anything, including his fellow angelic beings, that got in the way. He was willing to destroy goodness and truth and life too.

He knows he's a created being that is no match for the Creator. And he hates that. But more, he fears it.

To this day, he uses chaos to turn as many as he can from the Creator. He desperately wants us to allow the external chaos into our internal being. And in that fog, he hopes to reshape us into chaotic beings who will be carriers of his fallen nature.

Earlier, I quoted the first half of John 10:10. Now let's look at the whole thing.

> The thief comes only to steal and kill and destroy; I have come that they may have life, and have it to the full. (John 10:10 NIV)

Imagine a new neighbor moves into the house next to yours. He stops by and announces, "I just wanted you to know my goal is to steal, kill, and destroy everyone and everything on your property. That's all for now. Good-bye."

Would you shrug as you close the door, assuming he was just being dramatic? Perhaps he had a bad day and needed to vent. Or would you do everything possible to guard your home from this destructive being?

Then your doorbell rings again. This time it's the new neighbor on the other side. His introduction is equally unexpected, but exponentially better. "I moved into the neighborhood to help you experience life to the full." Then he adds with a wink, "I'll be keeping an eye on your other neighbor. He's a chaotic fellow."

How would knowing that about your neighbors change how you lived? How does knowing the contrast in John 10:10 change how you view the enemy's intent and that of Jesus?

Why does chaos almost always seek to infuse us with fear? Because everything the enemy does is rooted in death and fear. Everything that God, Jesus, and the Holy Spirit does is rooted in life and love.

And love is always stronger. According to 1 John 4:18, perfect love drives out fear. God is love, perfect love. Fear is flawed. And perfect love always drives out imperfect fear.

At the end of the day, every choice ever made—if you take it deep enough down the rabbit hole—comes from either love or fear. It seems the opposite of love would be hate. But there is something deeper, more primal, fueling the hate. That something is fear.

Fear-based responses don't always look like fear. Nor

is hate the only option. Fear can also come out as passivity, panic, impatience, jealously, offense, rage, regret, arrogance, control, or resignation. These external emotions or attitudes can look radically different, but the common denominator is that the one reacting in this way fears something. And from that place of fear, the person responds in brokenness.

Though they may not realize it, people who react in fear have allowed chaos in. Now, they release fear into the atmosphere. Knowingly or unknowingly, they have become agents of chaos.

Transforming humanity into agents of chaos is part of the enemy's plan. Though he's eager to destroy us, he also seeks to use us as weapons against God and his creation. He does this, in part, by baiting us to drink in the external chaos around us. We see an extreme result of this in the book of Ezekiel, where the prophet refers to the Pharaoh of Egypt as a mythical chaos-like sea monster (29:3-4).

It's a vicious circle that, once allowed in, feeds on itself and everyone involved.

It's like riding on the back of a tiger,

thinking it is your pet.

When actually, you are its lunch.

Building Their Throne on a Hurricane

In Genesis 1, God names the days of creation as good.

But he never named chaos as good. Ever. Neither should we.

Chaos wants us to believe we are random accidents as void and empty as it is. Creation reminds us we are wonderfully, beautifully, purposefully made beings filled with life.

Here's an interesting question. What does chaos create?

Well, nothing. Chaos can't.

It can't fill you. It is vast emptiness looking to consume you.

It can't produce love. It is saturated with fear.

It can't exhibit grace or kindness. Its essence is violent and abrasive.

It can't lead to abundance. Destruction leads to greater scarcity.

It can't birth new things. It seeks to end things.

Don't look to chaos to cure anything. It is the biggest cancer of all. It is a destructive force. It desecrates creation. It doesn't integrate. It dis-integrates. Disorder never leads to order. Scarcity never leads to abundance. Hate never leads to love.

What follows in the wake of chaos? Almost always,

what comes next is an attempt to seize control by the very ones who actively caused—or passively allowed—the chaos to occur. But control never leads to freedom.

Those who think they can use chaos to their personal benefit are wrong. Too late, they discover they were never the master of chaos. They tried to build their throne on a hurricane of instability, lay their foundation in an earthquake. It never works.

The chaos they seek to master will master them. The destruction they try to control will destroy them. Those who thought they could use it will find themselves used and abandoned. Scripture and the ash heap of history bear this out.

It's like riding on the back of a tiger, thinking it is your pet. When actually, you are its lunch.

No Fear

All this talk about the origin of chaos can be, well, a bit daunting.

The simple definition of chaos being a state of utter confusion or disorder was bad enough.

But this ancient view of chaos being intentional takes us out of the frying pan and into the fire. Things heat up when we realize the goal of chaos is not simply confusion but something far more personal.

We're at the halfway point in our journey. In the hero's journey, this moment is often referred to as the abyss or pit. The place where it seems things can't get worse. Where all hope seems lost.

But it's also the place of death and rebirth. So stay hopeful. This is the point where we can put fear to death and experience a rebirth of hope and life. Through God's love.

In the meantime, the enemy wants us to be overwhelmed. He wants us to drop our weapons without a fight. To doubt God's ability to come through or have good plans for us. The enemy is an accuser.

He accuses God to us:

> Now the serpent was more crafty than any of the wild animals the Lord God had made. He said to the woman, "Did God really say, 'You must not eat from any tree in the garden'?"

> The woman said to the serpent, "We may eat fruit from the trees in the garden, but God did say, 'You must not eat fruit from the tree that is in the middle of the garden, and you must not touch it, or you will die.'"
>
> "You will not certainly die," the serpent said to the woman. "For God knows that when you eat from it your eyes will be opened, and you will be like God, knowing good and evil." (Genesis 3:1–5 NIV)

And he accuses us to God:

> For the accuser of our brothers and sisters, who accuses them before our God day and night, has been hurled down. (Revelation 12:10 NIV)

But it won't work. Not if we stay close to God and refuse to let chaos in. Listen to this promise:

> Submit yourselves, then, to God. Resist the devil, and he will flee from you. (James 4:7 NIV)

The enemy *must* flee when we resist him. But we have to resist.

When it comes to chaos, we have to choose not to let it in.

Yes, the enemy is a roaring lion looking for those to devour (1 Peter 5:8). He wants us to live in fear, to believe all hope is lost and that our time is short. But he's the only one on borrowed time. In the book of Luke, Jesus describes how he "saw Satan fall like lightning from heaven" (10:18 NIV).

Satan is consumed with rage. Why?

> He is filled with fury, because he knows that his time is short. (Revelation 12:12 NIV)

Yet the Creator has all the time in the world. He created time. And he has never once worried about chaos. Jesus faced it in various forms throughout his ministry, and he overcome it every time with love and power.

Chaos is temporal but God is eternal. Chaos didn't get the first word, nor does it get the last.

Only God does.

> I am the First and the Last;
> there is no other God. (Isaiah 44:6 NLT)

> "I am the Alpha and the Omega—
> the beginning and the end," says the Lord God.
> (Revelation 1:8 NLT)

The very worst chaos can do is not too much for God. One day, the enemy and his chaos will be cut down, wholly and completely defeated (Revelation 20:10). At that time, God will then make all things new (Revelation 21:5).

The one that has been so opposed to the Creator, creation, and our God-given creativity will have no place in this new creation.

God and his sons and daughters are eternal. Chaos is not. Love is eternal. Fear is not.

These have been the hardest miles of our journey, but we've made it. Now it's time to turn a corner. Up ahead is a lake shimmering with light and life.

As the terrain shifts, so does our focus. We're leaving

the enemy behind. Our focus now turns to the brilliance of the Creator and how he approaches, disarms, and transforms chaos.

The one that has been so opposed
to the Creator, creation,
and our God-given creativity
will have no place
in this new creation.

Chaos is temporal
but God is eternal.
Chaos didn't get the first word,
nor does it get the last.
Only God does.

When chaos and the Creator
come face-to-face,
chaos blinks every time.

4

CREATOR

In a contest between love and fear,
I sometimes doubt love
is strong enough to win.
I worry that in direct combat,
love may get its tail kicked.
Thankfully, Scripture reminds me
that nothing is more powerful
than love.

The Power of Love

We've come to the perfect place to pause and catch our breath. Go ahead. Kick your shoes off. Let the water from the lake cool your feet. Lean back in the lush grass. Feel the warmth of the sun and the gentle breeze wash over you.

Remember, God is right here with us. He's been here the entire time, of course, both as the sage and the hero of our journey. But now we turn our focus to him.

He wants us to know him more fully. That's where we're headed now.

But first, he invites us to lighten our load. To release the remaining baggage we've been carrying all this way. God's not talking about what's in our backpacks. But rather what's weighing down our hearts, minds, and souls—whether it's the chaos of the world, the schemes of the enemy, or the fear trying to get in.

That resonates with me. In a contest between love and fear, I sometimes doubt love is strong enough to win. I mean, love is great. But fear plays dirty. It's a street brawler. And love is so . . . kind. I worry that in direct combat, love may get its tail kicked. Then what?

Thankfully, Scripture reminds me my concern is unfounded. Nothing is more powerful than love.

> For I am convinced that nothing can ever separate us from his love. Death can't, and life can't. The

> angels won't, and all the powers of hell itself cannot keep God's love away. Our fears for today, our worries about tomorrow, or where we are—high above the sky, or in the deepest ocean—nothing will ever be able to separate us from the love of God demonstrated by our Lord Jesus Christ when he died for us. (Romans 8:38–39 TLB)

All of creation must operate within those parameters. There are no exceptions. Not for death, life, politicians, movements, the outcast or the elite. Not for social media celebrities or those operating in the shadows. There are no loopholes for angels, demons, or the powers of hell. Nor for yesterday's mistakes, today's fears, or tomorrow's worries. Even the place you live, no matter how shaken it has become, has to give way to God.

God spoke the first word. God gets the last word.

Remember: God is eternal. Chaos is not. When chaos and the Creator come face-to-face, chaos blinks every time. In this world we will have trouble. But Jesus has overcome the world. Chaos may be inevitable, but God is invincible.

So before we start up again, leave whatever is troubling you behind. No matter how long you've carried that burden, it has no power to separate you from the mighty love of God.

There's no contest. God wins every time . . . through the power of love.

Knowing God As Creator

If you want to know a creator, look at what he or she creates.

You don't have to be close friends with your favorite songwriter or best-selling author to know their worldviews. Just sample their art. It reveals far more about their beliefs than they may realize.

If you want to know God, a good starting place is to consider his creation. The first way God makes himself known is as Creator. Through his creativity, we see his invisible qualities—his power and nature.

> For ever since the world was created, people have seen the earth and sky. Through everything God made, they can clearly see his invisible qualities—his eternal power and divine nature. So they have no excuse for not knowing God. (Romans 1:20 NLT)

How does God create? Extravagantly. Wildly. Freely. He didn't need time to warm up or find his groove. He wasn't searching for a formula or hoping nervously that others would approve of his creation.

He creates from a place of truth. Creation flows from who he is (his identity) and what he does (his creativity). In that sense, the vast panorama of creation reflects his essence—or presence—in endless ways.

> By his Son, God created the world in the beginning, and it will all belong to the Son at the end. This Son perfectly mirrors God, and is stamped with God's nature. He holds everything together by what he says—powerful words! (Hebrews 1:2–3 MSG)

Wouldn't you love to have witnessed the time of creation? God wasn't alone. Jesus was there. The Spirit was active. What do you think the mood was like? Was the process stressful, with God grimacing and struggling to make the ocean? Irritated the mountains weren't angled quite right. And the platypus? *Oops. Let's give that one another try.* Or was it a joyful, wild experience?

We don't have to guess. God doesn't just tell us what he created, he describes the atmosphere and mood as he did so. Let's join him there . . . in the beginning.

If you want to know a creator,
look at what he or she creates.

How does God create?
Extravagantly. Wildly. Freely.
He didn't need time to warm up
or find his groove.
He wasn't searching for a formula
or hoping nervously that others
would approve of his creation.

The Dance of Creation

Imagine being with God at the birth of our universe. Imagine the first stars, the wildflowers, the stallions, the oceans, humpback whales, ladybugs, redwood trees, snowflakes, and waterfalls.

Do these creations strike you as the works of a hesitant creator?

Proverbs 8 gives us an intimate glimpse of creation through the personification of Lady Wisdom. Notice how the creation process resembles a dance of delight far more than grueling work.

> In the beginning I was there,
> for God possessed me even before he created
> the universe.
> From eternity past I was set in place,
> before the world began.
> I was anointed from the beginning.
> Before the oceans depths were poured out,
> and before there were any glorious fountains
> overflowing with water,
> I was there, dancing!
> Even before one mountain had been sculpted
> or one hill raised up,
> I was already there, dancing!

When he created the earth, the fields,
even the first atom of dust,
I was already there.
When he hung the tapestry of the heavens
and stretched out the horizon of the earth,
when the clouds and skies were set in place
and the subterranean fountains began to flow
strong,
I was already there.
when he set in place the pillars of the earth
and spoke the decrees of the seas,
commanding the waves
so that they wouldn't overstep their boundaries,
I was there, close to the Creator's side as his
master artist.
Daily he was filled with delight in me
as I playfully rejoiced before him.
I laughed and played,
so happy with what he had made,
while finding my delight in the children of men
(Proverbs 8:22–31 TPT)

So much is happening here.

Wisdom was already with God. She was there from eternity, before the world began.

During creation, Lady Wisdom is right there at God's side. She refers to him as a master artist filled with delight. Creation was—and is—the antidote to chaos. It filled the void with beauty, purpose, life, and order.

Notice how wisdom is described. Not as some stuffy professor or elderly protector of dusty books full of rigid rules and stale formulas.

Lady Wisdom is vibrant. Playful. Laughing. Rejoicing. Delighted.

Is that how you view God's wisdom? He created wisdom before he created this world. And this atmosphere of wonder, joy, and awe was present in creation.

C. S. Lewis offers this imaginary, fantastical look at the world's creation in *The Magician's Nephew*[1] from his masterful series The Chronicles of Narnia:

> In the darkness, something was happening at last. A voice had begun to sing. It was very far away and Digory found it hard to decide from which direction it was coming. Sometimes it seemed to come from all directions at once. Sometimes he almost thought it was coming out of the earth beneath them. Its lower notes were deep enough to be the voice of the earth herself. There were no words. There was hardly even a tune. But it was, beyond comparison the most beautiful noise he had ever heard. It was so beautiful he could hardly bear it . . . . Then two wonders happened at the same moment. One was that the voice was suddenly joined by other voices; more voices than you could possibly count. They were in harmony with it, but far higher up the scale: cold, tingling, silvery voices. The second wonder was that the blackness overhead, all at once, was blazing with stars. They didn't come out gently one by one, as they do on a summer evening. One moment there had been nothing but darkness; next moment a thousand, thousand points of light leaped out—single stars,

1. *The Magician's Nephew*, by C.S. Lewis, HarperCollins.

constellations, and planets, brighter and bigger than any in our world.

In this fictionalized account, darkness is penetrated by a voice. A singing voice. The voice of the great lion, Aslan. Then his voice is joined by other voices. And from that song, creation begins. With a creative roar.

Everything about God's creation was filled with intention, light and life. All of it overflowed with the trueness, wisdom, and goodness of God.

It's helpful to remember that our story began with God's breathtaking creativity.

Everything That's Anything

God is the uncreated Creator. He has always existed as Father, Son, and Holy Spirit.

There is no time when God wasn't. He precedes everything . . . including time.

Let's take a moment and savor a few of the things he created from nothing.

Heaven	Angels	Jalapeños	Saturn
Photons	Time	Cheetahs	Turtles
Blue	Water	Hummingbirds	Honeysuckle
Cherries	Ocean	Curiosity	Forest
Fields	Stars	Story	Imagination
Beauty	Color	Music	Dance
Entropy	Adventure	Love	Hope
Birth	Worship	Family	Echoes
Freedom	Creativity	Sleep	Dreams
Gravity	Memory	Sight	Faith
Fireflies	Echoes	Touch	Humor

Before any of these things came to be, they existed in the mind of God. He thought of them and then spoke them into being.

Neither humans nor our enemy can bring anything into existence from nothing. Chaos talks a good game.

But it is always reactionary. Whatever God is doing, it tries to undo. God begins a new creation. Chaos tries an old tactic to defuse its impact. God ignites sparks of love and light across the cosmos and chaos tries to catch up. Yet God is always light-years ahead of it. And not by just a little. But by a gap that spans, as Buzz Lightyear might say, to infinity and beyond.

Everything that is anything exists because God chooses to bring his ideas to life.

Everything that is anything
exists because God chooses
to bring his ideas to life.

Nothing about God is static.

Even his name is an ongoing verb.

Creation Continues

Did God stop creating after the Genesis creation?

I mean, if you want to quit at the top of your game, the climax of the Genesis creation would be a good place to accept your award, take a bow, and retire as Creator.

But not God. He is the continual Creator.

How is he creating today? Here are a few examples:

> Create in me a new, clean heart, O God, filled with clean thoughts and right desires. (Psalm 51:10 TLB)

> Therefore, if anyone is in Christ, the new creation has come: The old has gone, the new is here! (2 Corinthians 5:17 NIV)

> For see, I am creating new heavens and a new earth—so wonderful that no one will even think about the old ones anymore. (Isaiah 65:17 TLB)

Do you view God's creativity as something that happened primarily in the past, or as actively bringing new ideas and plans and hearts to life now? Nothing about God is static. Even his name is an ongoing verb. The name Yahweh conveys simultaneous aspects of past, present, and future. It is built on the Hebrew verb "to be"—which connotes eternal, ongoing existence.

> "I am the Alpha and the Omega—the beginning and the end," says the Lord God. "I am the one who is, who always was, and who is still to come—the Almighty One." (Revelation 1:8 NLT)

Maybe that's why when Moses asks who he should say sent him, God simply replies "I AM WHO I AM" (Exodus 3:14 NLT).

Perhaps we should follow the psalmist's lead and increase our awe of the Creator:

> The world's a huge stockpile
> of God-wonders and God-thoughts.
> Nothing and no one
> comes close to you!
> I start talking about you, telling what I know,
> and quickly run out of words.
> Neither numbers nor words
> account for you.
> Doing something for you, bringing something to
> you—
> that's not what you're after.
> Being religious, acting pious—
> that's not what you're asking for.
> You've opened my ears
> so I can listen. (Psalm 40:4–6 MSG)

The Creator is continuously creating. Ask him to show you ways to join the dance.

Knowing God As Father

The first way God introduces himself is as Creator. But I believe one of the favorite ways God loves to be known is as Father.

He is the Father of Light.

> Every desirable and beneficial gift comes out of heaven. The gifts are rivers of light cascading down from the Father of Light. There is nothing deceitful in God, nothing two-faced, nothing fickle. He brought us to life using the true Word, showing us off as the crown of all his creatures. (James 1:17–18 MSG)

He is the Father of creation, of truth, of life . . . and of us.

God breathed life into Adam and soon after created Eve. Throughout Scripture, we see God as a good, adoring, attentive, boundlessly creative Father.

Here's how the psalmist describes our relationship to God:

> For you created my inmost being;
> you knit me together in my mother's womb.
> I praise you because I am fearfully and wonderfully made;

> your works are wonderful,
> I know that full well.
> My frame was not hidden from you
> when I was made in the secret place,
> when I was woven together in the depths of the earth.
> Your eyes saw my unformed body;
> all the days ordained for me were written in your book
> before one of them came to be.
> (Psalm 139:13–16 NIV)

> Long before he laid down earth's foundations, he had us in mind, had settled on us as the focus of his love, to be made whole and holy by his love. (Ephesians 1:4 MSG)

And here's how God describes his relationship to us:

> I will be a Father to you, and you will be my sons and daughters. (2 Corinthians 6:18)

He creates. And then he fathers.

Knowing God as Creator is so essential. If he were a distant, remote, checked-out Creator, we might still be in awe. But it would be impossible to experience intimacy with him. The reason we can is because he also chooses to love us as a father loves his sons and daughters. Every part of our identity, including our creativity, flows from that love.

When we enter into our days together with God, we can know indescribable joy and peace. The expectancy of waking up each day wondering what our Father has for us is so much richer than striving to make our expectations happen.

> This resurrection life you received from God is not a timid, grave-tending life. It's adventurously expectant, greeting God with a childlike "What's next, Papa?" God's Spirit touches our spirits and confirms who we really are. We know who he is, and we know who we are: Father and children. (Romans 8:15–16 MSG)

Though chaos tries to make us forget or doubt who we are, when we know God as Father, we know our true identity—sons and daughters who co-create with our dad.

Though chaos tries to make us
forget or doubt who we are,
when we know God as Father,
we know our true identity—
sons and daughters who
co-create with our dad.

Nobody Does It Better

If you could spend time with the top creative genius in your field, would you do so?

We often look to role models to challenge our thinking about what is possible. And that can be helpful, whether we are seeking peers, exemplars of our profession, or heroes of our faith.

But we often forget to look to God as our prime example.

Have you considered that God *is* the ultimate expert of the very thing you're drawn to? Nobody knows more about what you love to do than the Creator of everything. He has infused you with your interests and talents so you can pursue them *with* him. Your gifting is not just a talent...it is an invitation.

He isn't after just what you have to offer. He's after your heart. He wants to spend time with you. In the very things he stirred you to run after.

Listen to the intimacy of his words:

> I don't want your sacrifices—I want your love; I don't want your offerings—I want you to know me. (Hosea 6:6 TLB)

Have you ever wondered why God longs for us to know him as Creator and Father?

Could it be that he's far more interested in doing life with us than in what we do for him? That's what the verse in Hosea seems to imply. And it works both ways. How would things shift if our greatest hunger was to know God more intimately rather than asking him to do more for us? He wants our love more than anything else we could do for him or give him.

The Creator has set love above everything else.

> Three things will last forever—faith, hope, and love—and the greatest of these is love. (1 Corinthians 13:13 NLT)

That is how creation was originally designed. And now God invites us to help restore creation. To do so, we must know God as Creator and Father. When we do, we can actively pursue our lives, dreams, and gifting as sons and daughters with a Creative Father. It is his invitation into intimacy, through the doorway of initiation.

The Origin of Creativity

We've looked at the origin of chaos. Now let's turn to the origin of creativity.

Not creativity as defined by humans or institutions past or present. Creativity isn't determined by a degree or reserved for the elite to bestow as they please. You don't need to win an award to prove you're creative.

Humans aren't the original creators or the official gatekeepers of creativity. God is.

So let's pursue creativity from God's perspective. Where does he give us our first glimpse of creativity? From the very moment we are introduced to him. Genesis begins with God creating. It's the first sentence of Scripture. The opening story we enter into.

Given that, do you think creativity might have a deeper, more essential role in our lives and our world than we've dared imagine? That's a good question to ponder as we keep moving forward.

Humans aren't the original creators
or the official gatekeepers
of creativity.
God is.

Double Vision

Are you aware that the Genesis creation story isn't the only account of creation in Scripture?

It is retold from a different perspective in the New Testament.

It's fascinating to read the first verses of the books of Genesis and John back-to-back. Though both start with the words, "In the beginning," John's account veers into new territory with some "behind the scenes" details about creation.

In Genesis 1:1–3 we read:

> In the beginning God created the heavens and the earth. Now the earth was formless and empty, darkness was over the surface of the deep, and the Spirit of God was hovering over the waters. And God said, "Let there be light," and there was light. (NIV)

John 1:1–10 expresses it this way:

> In the beginning was the Word, and the Word was with God, and the Word was God. He was with God in the beginning. Through him all things were made; without him nothing was made that has been made. In him was life, and that life was the light of all mankind. The light shines in the darkness, and the darkness has not overcome it.

> There was a man sent from God whose name was John. He came as a witness to testify concerning that light, so that through him all might believe. He himself was not the light; he came only as a witness to the light.
>
> The true light that gives light to everyone was coming into the world. He was in the world, and though the world was made through him, the world did not recognize him. (NIV)

In John's version, we see the essential role Jesus played in creation. Through him *all* things were made. *Nothing* was made without him. His life is described as the light of all humanity. Other translations say the darkness did not comprehend this light (NKJV) or can never extinguish it (TLB). The Message says it even more strikingly: "The Life-Light blazed out of the darkness; the darkness couldn't put it out."

His light shines in the darkness and the darkness cannot overcome it.

At the start of our journey, we saw how Jesus gave us a heads-up that in this world there will be trouble. Then he told us to take heart, because he has overcome the world (John 16:33). We can overcome what comes against us because Jesus has overcome the darkness with his light. He has overcome the world with his presence. Through him, we can be overcomers.

In John's version,
we see the essential role
Jesus played in creation.
Through him *all* things were made.
Nothing was made without him.

The best creativity,
according to the Creator,
is always done in collaboration—
not isolation.

The Ways of Creation

In Genesis 1 we see the Creator in his glory. So much happens in these first six movements of creation.

On the first day, God begins by speaking.

> And God said, "Let there be light," and there was light. (Genesis 1:3 NIV)

The first thing to note is that God didn't create alone.

> In the beginning was the Word, and the Word was with God, and the Word was God. He was with God in the beginning. (John 1:1–2 NIV)

The Word who was with God is Jesus. Jesus was with God from the beginning. Creation was accomplished by creative fellowship—Father, Son, and Holy Spirit. The trinity. Together.

Creation wasn't a solo project. It was a generous cooperative mission.

God created. The Spirit was brooding over the chaos (Genesis 1:2). Jesus was the conduit through which everything was made.

> Through him all things were made; without him nothing was made that has been made. In him was life, and that life was the light of all mankind.

> The light shines in the darkness, and the darkness has not overcome it. (John 1:3–5 NIV)

Remember Lady Wisdom's joy in the creation process (Proverbs 8)? While this poem personifies wisdom, it also reveals the fellowship in creation. I wonder what role the angelic beings were given. It's hard to imagine God heading out to begin his creation project and telling the angelic beings to stay behind. "I'll let you know what happened when I get back!"

God wasn't on a solo creative mission then—nor is he now. We, as his sons and daughters, are invited to co-create with him in this moment.

The best creativity, according to the Creator, is always done in collaboration—not isolation.

The Days of Creation

On the first day of creation, God spoke light into existence. Not the sun, but light itself. As we're told in John 1:4–5, Jesus is the light of all mankind. The light shines in the darkness, and the darkness has not overcome it.

We can't look directly at the sun even with high intensity sunglasses. Imagine how intense this light would be.

But God, through Jesus, illuminated our world with pure light. He saw that it was good and then separated light from darkness, naming the light *day*.

Regardless of what was being created, the overall pattern in the days of creation is that God speaks, he sees, he separates, and he names.

In the following days, he creates everything that is anything. After light comes sky. Then seeds of every kind of plant and tree. Sea. Sun. Moon. Stars. Birds above. Fish below. Great and small beasts roaming the land. And a unique garden. Tended to by God. Prepared as the home of man and woman.

The Creator infuses every living creature with life. He does the same for ocean, sky, and all the plants and trees. In varying ways, seen and unseen, creation is alive. And its life originates with God. And through Jesus. With the Spirit actively present.

This wasn't an impersonal, remote creation process. God was fully present. This was intimate, up-close creation. God literally breathed life into Adam.

There was order to creation. An order to the process. A trueness to how and what he created.

It wasn't chaotic. Nor was it formulaic. God didn't recreate the same thing every day. It was a new dance each time. Unique. Distinct.

For some, *order* may hold a negative connotation, like a drill sergeant ordering you to do something you don't want to do. That's not what *order* means in this context. Think of order here as the way things were meant to be. Purpose. Design. Intention.

Each part of creation had never been . . . until it was. It all began with God speaking.

And he still speaks. He still creates.

A Genesis Week . . . in Me

Listen to this powerful request the psalmist makes to God:

> God, make a fresh start in me,
> shape a Genesis week from the chaos of my life.
> (Psalm 51:10 MSG)

The psalmist's pleas are our plea. *God, give us a fresh start. Relief from the chaos. Hope for the future. A new beginning. Turn the disorder to order . . . within us.*

How might he do that?

Through a Genesis week. This phrase doesn't just signify a minor improvement to our situation. It compares the greatest act of creation we can imagine to what God can do within us.

He can bring life into the empty, void places in us through his extravagant, abundant creativity.

That's what we're after.

Yes, God! Shape a Genesis week from the chaos of our lives.

God, make a fresh start in me,
shape a Genesis week from
the chaos of my life.
(Psalm 51:10 MSG)

A Pause to Savor

Then comes the seventh day. The day we say God rested.

What does that mean? Why would he rest? God wasn't exhausted. He didn't work up a sweat. He could have created every day for millions of years and never repeated himself. Every day another new creation.

Mark Twain is said to have made this wry observation about creation: "Man was made at the end of the week's work, when God was tired." That says more about humanity than God. But the part about God isn't accurate.

Isaiah reminds us:

> Do you not know?
> Have you not heard?
> The Lord is the everlasting God,
> the Creator of the ends of the earth.
> He will not grow tired or weary,
> and his understanding no one can fathom.
> He gives strength to the weary
> and increases the power of the weak.
> (Isaiah 40:28–29 NIV)

God wasn't tired. He had the same full strength after the days of creation that he had before he began. And has endless reserves of strength and power to give to anyone who needs it.

But he did treat the seventh day uniquely.

I believe God was taking time to savor his creativity and to model for us what our rhythm of work, worship, and restoration should look like.

Here's perhaps a better way to understand it: God took in all that he had made . . . and engaged it. He enjoyed it. He stopped doing more, at least momentarily, because he was content and pleased with the magnificence of what he'd done.

Then God blessed the seventh day and made it holy, because on it he rested from all the work of creating that he had done. (Genesis 2:3 NIV)

He blessed it. He made it holy. He paused from creating. And he proclaimed it good.

He savored his creation.

God's Response to Chaos

God opposes chaos. Not some of the time. But every time it tries to strike.

He opposed it when it appeared in Lucifer's heart. He fought it during the rebellion in heaven. His Spirit transformed the murky emptiness of Genesis 1:2. He provided a rescue for humanity when the serpent entered into the garden and created chaos there.

The void continuously tries to overcome us. But in every clash, God overcomes it.

The prophet Isaiah gives us this insight:

> For the Lord is God,
> and he created the heavens and earth
> and put everything in place.
> He made the world to be lived in,
> not to be a place of empty chaos.
> "I am the Lord," he says,
> "and there is no other." (45:18 NLT)

But the battle against chaos remains. In the book of Jeremiah, we hear the prophet's vision of coming disaster. Notice the close association to chaos.

> I looked at the earth—
> it was back to pre-Genesis chaos and emptiness.

> I looked at the skies,
> and not a star to be seen. (Jeremiah 4:23 MSG)

Yet later in this same chapter, we hear the prophet compare the certainty of Israel's stability with the ongoing order of the cosmos.

> "If this ordered cosmos ever fell to pieces,
> fell into chaos before me"—God's Decree—
> "Then and only then might Israel fall apart
> and disappear as a nation before me."
> (Jeremiah 31:36 MSG)

Isaiah reminds us of God's heroic victories over chaos. In the following passage, the name Rahab refers to the primeval Leviathan.

> Wake up, wake up, flex your muscles, God!
> Wake up as in the old days, in the long ago.
> Didn't you once make mincemeat of Rahab,
> dispatch the old chaos-dragon?
> And didn't you once dry up the sea,
> the powerful waters of the deep,
> And then made the bottom of the ocean a road
> for the redeemed to walk across?
> (Isaiah 51:9–10 MSG)

Though the enemy's goal is to use chaos to steal, kill, and destroy (John 10:10), the Bible shows us what will happen:

> Then death and the grave were thrown into the lake of fire. (Revelation 20:14 NLT)

Neither the enemy nor chaos will survive this. One day, their time will come to a definitive end.

Can there be any doubt what God thinks about chaos—or his absolute victory over it?

The void continuously tries

to overcome us.

But in every clash,

God overcomes it.

Chaos Pours Out of the Skies

How does chaos tend to play out across our world today? Surprisingly, not much different than it did thousands of years ago.

> Earth is polluted by its very own people,
> who have broken its laws,
> Disrupted its order,
> violated the sacred and eternal covenant.
> Therefore a curse, like a cancer,
> ravages the earth.
> Its people pay the price of their sacrilege.
> They dwindle away, dying out one by one.
> No more wine, no more vineyards,
> no more songs or singers.
> The laughter of castanets is gone,
> the shouts of celebrants, gone,
> the laughter of fiddles, gone.
> No more parties with toasts of champagne.
> Serious drinkers gag on their drinks.
> The chaotic cities are unlivable. Anarchy reigns.
> Every house is boarded up, condemned.
> People riot in the streets for wine,
> but the good times are gone forever—

no more joy for this old world.
The city is dead and deserted,
bulldozed into piles of rubble.
That's the way it will be on this earth.
This is the fate of all nations:
An olive tree shaken clean of its olives,
a grapevine picked clean of its grapes.
(Isaiah 24:5–13 MSG)

It's hard to read. The situation seems hopeless. And the similarities to our current problems are startling.

Even in such dire times, the prophet offers a glimmer of hope:

But there are some who will break into glad song.
Out of the west they'll shout of God's majesty.
Yes, from the east God's glory will ascend.
Every island of the sea
Will broadcast God's fame,
the fame of the God of Israel.
From the four winds and the seven seas we hear
the singing: "All praise to the Righteous One!"
(Isaiah 24:14–16 MSG)

Yet Isaiah can't help himself. He remains skeptical:

But I said, "That's all well and good for somebody,
but all I can see is doom, doom, and more doom."
All of them at one another's throats,
yes, all of them at one another's throats.
Terror and pits and booby traps
are everywhere, whoever you are.

If you run from the terror,
you'll fall into the pit.
If you climb out of the pit,
you'll get caught in the trap.
Chaos pours out of the skies.
The foundations of earth are crumbling.
Earth is smashed to pieces,
earth is ripped to shreds,
earth is wobbling out of control,
Earth staggers like a drunk,
sways like a shack in a high wind.
Its piled-up sins are too much for it.
It collapses and won't get up again.
(Isaiah 24:16–20 MSG)

In spite of how hopeless things look from the human perspective, we see God's decisive victory over the chaos that's pouring out of the sky. Notice that our hope doesn't rest in humanity doing right, but in God being God.

That's when God will call on the carpet
rebel powers in the skies and
Rebel kings on earth.
They'll be rounded up like prisoners in a jail,
Corralled and locked up in a jail,
and then sentenced and put to hard labor.
Shamefaced moon will cower, humiliated,
red-faced sun will skulk, disgraced,
Because God-of-the-Angel-Armies will take over,
ruling from Mount Zion and Jerusalem,
Splendid and glorious
before all his leaders. (Isaiah 24:21–23 MSG)

Chaos isn't an Old Testament problem. It's a human problem. Listen to how Paul describes the chaos of his times:

> Since they thought it foolish to acknowledge God, he abandoned them to their foolish thinking and let them do things that should never be done. Their lives became full of every kind of wickedness, sin, greed, hate, envy, murder, quarreling, deception, malicious behavior, and gossip. They are backstabbers, haters of God, insolent, proud, and boastful. They invent new ways of sinning, and they disobey their parents. They refuse to understand, break their promises, are heartless, and have no mercy. They know God's justice requires that those who do these things deserve to die, yet they do them anyway. Worse yet, they encourage others to do them, too. (Romans 1:28–32 NLT)

Unfortunately, this sounds pretty much like the summary of the local and global events we wake up to each day.

God makes clear what happens to those who choose life without him. They quite literally lose their ability to make wise decisions. Those that leave God behind and let chaos in become agents of chaos.

Yet though this world is shaken, God isn't.

But what about us? What are we to do?

Us

God has continually and creatively dealt with chaos, from overcoming the rebellion in heaven to creating the cosmos where there had been an empty void.

But there's another way he counters chaos that we haven't yet addressed.

He created us. He chose his sons and daughters to be his intimate allies in overcoming chaos.

Though we were made in the image of God, that was marred by the fall of Adam and Eve.

Our original design was tainted in the fall. We took beauty, life, and order and traded it for a void that we sought to fill on our own.

But God doesn't just create. He recreates. And he is intent on restoring our original design.

Just as God entered the chaos of Genesis 1:2, he enters our internal and external chaos and brings order to it. Not order as in "get your act together!" But order as in things being brought back to how they were meant to be. How we were meant to be.

We were created to walk with the Creator in the cool of the garden. But Adam and Eve turned their back on God's design. They doubted God and took matters into their own hands, which always ushers in chaos. That's the temptation. If God is holding out, then life really is all up to us.

In the storms of life, as the waters are rising, God wants to show us how to overcome. And he does so in ways that are never quite the same as the time before.

Look at the many ways God uses the same substance—water—in endlessly creative ways.

Is God inviting us to walk on it today (Matthew 14:28–29)? Or turn the water into wine (John 2:7–9)? Perhaps he wants to part it and take us between two walls of water (Exodus 14:21–22)? Other times, he shows us how to calm the waves (Mark 4:39). There is no formula. We can't approach every situation the same way. We must ask.

Have you noticed that God rarely calls us into waters we can overcome in our own strength? He is most active in the deep, where the waters are over our head. Yet even then, the water is only overwhelming when we think it is up to us to navigate it.

He constantly shows us new ways to overcome what comes against us. But he never wants us to accept the chaos as our new normal. We weren't created for chaos. We were created to overcome it.

> The God who made the world and everything in it, this Master of sky and land, doesn't live in custom-made shrines or need the human race to run errands for him, as if he couldn't take care of himself. He makes the creatures; the creatures don't make him. Starting from scratch, he made the entire human race and made the earth hospitable, with plenty of time and space for living so we could seek after God, and not just grope around in the dark but actually *find* him. He doesn't play hide-and-seek with us. He's not remote; he's *near*. We live and move in him, can't get away from him! One of your poets said it well:

"We're the God-created." (Acts 17:24–29 MSG)

We, the God-created, have a role to play in this adventure of re-creation.

We, the God-created,
have a role to play in this
adventure of re-creation.

Jesus' Response to Chaos

When I first started researching in Scripture how Jesus responded to chaos, I was confident I'd find a few relevant examples. I underestimated by a long shot.

In pretty much every story, Jesus is overcoming some form of chaos. Which is why he can definitively say he's overcome the world (John 16:33). Sometimes the chaos involved people's motives or a force of nature. Other times, it involved encounters with demons, physical crises, people wanting to kill him, or the death of a friend. He continuously found ways to reshape disorder into order, fear into love, and death into life.

One of my favorite examples is when Jesus spoke calm to the wind and the waves.

> One day he and his disciples got in a boat. "Let's cross the lake," he said. And off they went. It was smooth sailing, and he fell asleep. A terrific storm came up suddenly on the lake. Water poured in, and they were about to capsize. They woke Jesus: "Master, Master, we're going to drown!"
>
> Getting to his feet, he told the wind, "Silence!" and the waves, "Quiet down!" They did it. The lake became smooth as glass.

> Then he said to his disciples, "Why can't you trust me?"
>
> They were in absolute awe, staggered and stammering, "Who is this, anyway? He calls out to the winds and sea, and they do what he tells them!" (Luke 8:22–25 MSG)

Notice that Jesus identified their fear ("we're going to drown!") as a trust issue. After he told the wind and water to calm down, he asked his disciples, "Why can't you trust me?"

Another example of Jesus confronting chaos involves a demon-possessed man. The man called himself (or the demons in him) a rioting mob. Jesus calmly but directly went after what had gotten into him. His focus was on getting the chaos within . . . out.

The man must have felt like the walking dead. He made his home among tombs and graves.

> They arrived on the other side of the sea in the country of the Gerasenes. As Jesus got out of the boat, a madman from the cemetery came up to him. He lived there among the tombs and graves. No one could restrain him—he couldn't be chained, couldn't be tied down. He had been tied up many times with chains and ropes, but he broke the chains, snapped the ropes. No one was strong enough to tame him. Night and day he roamed through the graves and the hills, screaming out and slashing himself with sharp stones.

> When he saw Jesus a long way off, he ran and bowed in worship before him—then bellowed in protest, "What business do you have, Jesus, Son of the High God, messing with me? I swear to God, don't give me a hard time!" (Jesus had just commanded the tormenting evil spirit, "Out! Get out of the man!")
>
> Jesus asked him, "Tell me your name."
>
> He replied, "My name is Mob. I'm a rioting mob." Then he desperately begged Jesus not to banish them from the country.
>
> A large herd of pigs was browsing and rooting on a nearby hill. The demons begged him, "Send us to the pigs so we can live in them." Jesus gave the order. But it was even worse for the pigs than for the man. Crazed, they stampeded over a cliff into the sea and drowned.
>
> Those tending the pigs, scared to death, bolted and told their story in town and country. Everyone wanted to see what had happened. They came up to Jesus and saw the madman sitting there wearing decent clothes and making sense, no longer a walking madhouse of a man. (Mark 5:1–15 MSG)

What did Jesus cast out of the man? Demons who described themselves here as "Mob." Other translations refer to them as "Legion," for they were many.

Again, whatever form chaos takes, its goal is to get

inside us—and then break us, control us, and hold us captive.

It's no coincidence Jesus defined his ministry in the way he did. When he was asked why he came, he referenced Isaiah 61, saying his mission was to heal the brokenhearted and set the captives free. He came to undo the damage of sin, chaos, and the evil one in our fallen world by restoring our hearts and setting us free.

In encounter after encounter, that's exactly what he did. He never ran from chaos or gave it a pass. Jesus purposely went into the wilderness for forty days of fasting and testing. Ultimately, he chose the chaos of death on a cross. And through that sacrifice, he forever defeated the enemy and his chaos.

Yes, for now, we still must contend with the enemy and chaos. For a time. But there is no question of the final outcome.

No matter how it tried, the darkness couldn't overcome the light. It still can't. It never will.

The Holy Spirit's Response to Chaos

What is your image of the Holy Spirit?

Some view the Spirit as a dove or bird largely due to two key passages.

In Genesis 1:2, God's Spirit is described as brooding, or spreading its wings like a bird, over the murky nothingness. This is meant to be a life-giving image, not a delicate one. It describes a bold act, the transforming of chaos and emptiness into life and order.

Then there's the story of the baptism of Jesus, where the Spirit descends from heaven to rest on Jesus like a dove (Luke 3:22).

Yes, the Spirit brings peace to chaos and blessings from the Father.

In addition, this more mysterious part of the Trinity is revealed to be a powerful, potent force. Acts 2 describes the Spirit as a mighty rushing wind and a tongue of wildfire that ignited the hearts of early believers. I don't think anyone present was viewing the Spirit as dovelike.

The Spirit is also named as the source of wisdom, the only one who can comprehend the very thoughts of God (1 Corinthians 2:11).

And the Spirit is actively involved in our lives today. As the Spirit of wisdom and understanding, counsel and might (Isaiah 11:2). And one who pours God's love into our hearts (Romans 5:5), intercedes for us when we lack words (Romans 8:26–27), and overcomes the spirit of fear in us with power, love, and self-control (2 Timothy 1:7). The Spirit helps us not give in to the desires of our flesh (Galatians 5:16) while setting us free from the law of sin and death (Romans 8:1–2).

In what Scripture calls "the last days" (which feel a lot like these days), God says:

> I will pour out my Spirit on all people.
> Your sons and daughters will prophesy,
> your young men will see visions,
> your old men will dream dreams. (Acts 2:17 NIV)

As the craziness rises, I believe the Spirit will communicate to us in ways that break through the confusion and tear down walls. These dreams, visions, and prophesies will reveal what is to come and, I believe, draw people back to the Creator.

The Spirit actively changes the atmosphere in this world and in our hearts for good. No matter how chaos tries to condemn, confine, or control us, the Spirit counters with the rushing wind and consuming fire of freedom.

> Now the Lord is the Spirit, and where the Spirit of the Lord is, there is freedom.
> (2 Corinthians 3:17 NIV)

The Holy Spirit is the antithesis of chaos, whether bringing life from the empty void in creation or transforming the empty places within us.

What Awaits

Through the Creator, we see the original intent for all creation. And we are given a better way to respond to chaos.

Notice how God, Jesus, and the Holy Spirit don't ever seem surprised when it appears. Nor do they wait it out, avoid it, accept it, or panic.

Considering all of that leaves me with one big thought: I absolutely love God.

I am stunned at his brilliant imagination. I savor the way he brings order from disorder. I'm in awe at how he created from his trueness, goodness, and generous abundance. I'm blown away by how he does whatever it takes to redeem his creation.

As we prepare to turn a corner to the next leg of our journey, let's remember these essential takeaways:

1. The reason God introduces himself as Creator in the first sentence of Scripture is because that identity speaks to a key aspect of who he is... and who we are. He is our Creator. We have his DNA within us. That means we have the opportunity to co-create with him.

2. The Spirit's first act in Scripture is to overcome chaos in Genesis 1:2. I believe that's because he knows we'll need to do the same. As it was then, the Spirit will be an essential part of this process.

3. Knowing God as Father allows us to know ourselves as sons and daughters. This allows our relationship with God to be based on being more rather than doing more.

4. God invites us to approach chaos as he does by responding to it through our presence and our creativity. He both invites us—and initiates us—to play our part in this story.

In every hero's journey, there comes a point where one must discover their special powers and learn to wield them. This is no different. We must shift from understanding the story we find ourselves in to stepping fully into the story.

Earlier I asked if perhaps creativity might have a deeper, more essential role in our world than we've dared imagine. I'm convinced the answer is yes.

But do you sense your creativity has been thwarted—or that you aren't creative at all? We'll now explore why God-given creativity is so opposed and the essential role it can play in overcoming chaos. I think you'll be astonished.

That is what awaits us.

5

UNSHAKEN OVERCOMERS

Have you ever considered
that we are continuing to
be created as we create?

Rethink Creativity

Now that we know what chaos is made of, let's see what we're made of.

Have you ever considered that we are continuing to be created as we create? The God who made us shapes us as we pursue the gifts he gave us, bringing us from disorder to order.

> Therefore, if anyone is in Christ, the new creation has come: The old has gone, the new is here!
> (2 Corinthians 5:17 NIV)

But what good is a new beginning if we are determined to stay the same? God didn't make us new creations just for us to return to chaos. The goal here is to step fully into your creativity as a new creation, neither underestimating its power nor overestimating your readiness.

As you start to see yourself in new ways, it's a good time to see creativity through a new lens.

Here's my definition of creativity.

> *God-infused creativity is using our presence and our gifting to bring something new into existence in a way that changes people and the atmosphere for good.*

Specifically, we bring beauty, life, and order where there was disorder and a void. If you think about it, that's how God created "in the beginning." Through his presence, or identity. And through his creativity.

Our creativity is a fusion of our unique presence and gifting. This is a huge concept. Because it includes everyone and excludes no one except those who refuse to enter into their gifting with God.

Seamstresses, deal makers, bakers, mechanics, electricians, students, teachers, stay-at-home parents, nurses, florists, baristas, ballerinas, flight attendants, personal trainers, and every one of us are creative. Creativity includes every occupation or interest. Known or unknown. Invented or yet to come. It could be your job. It could be a hobby. It could just be a dream . . . for now. All of it comes under the umbrella of God-infused creativity fueled by our presence and gifting.

Though your creative expression will be specific to you, there are no limits because God is limitless. Our "art" is how our gifting plays out. It's the "new" that we bring into existence.

The sons and daughters of God are artisans. We have the imagination of the Creator flowing in and through us. Our time in God's presence reshapes us, which in turn allows our creativity to reshape chaos.

A teacher's creativity brings understanding to complex topics. The way she teaches or shapes her students is the art. An architect is an expert at seeing a structure before it exists. The art is in making the structure a reality one brick or column at a time. A chef understands how various food and flavors come together. His art is the edible presentation on the plate. A coach is skilled at the knowledge of a particular sport. That is her gift. Her art is played out on the court based on how she shapes her team.

Creativity is what we do. Our *what*.

Art is what we make. Our *how*.

Before moving forward, we must first let go of something in the way. Our doubt.

The sons and daughters
of God are artisans.
We have the imagination of the
Creator flowing in and through us.
Our time in God's presence
reshapes us, which in turn allows
our creativity to reshape chaos.

You've Got to Be Kidding

Let's start here.

You. Are. Creative.

Pause and notice your reaction to those three words.

I'm guessing it was something like, "Creative? I'm not creative." Or, "You've got to be kidding. My creativity isn't valuable or worth fighting for. No one even notices it."

Why are many of us so quick to dismiss this significant aspect of our lives when chaos is so intentional at targeting it?

Fair question.

What I want to help you uncover here are the unique gifts you have inside you. Yes . . . you. If you haven't discovered this aspect of yourself yet, don't assume it isn't there. Though we often don't see ourselves as creative, we all are. How could anyone not be? We're all sons and daughters of the Creator. Our Father's DNA courses through our veins.

Creativity isn't limited to the few. The problem is that few invite the Creator into their creativity.

By the way, don't blame yourself for not feeling creative. The enemy works overtime to hide it from us, diminish it, and accuse us of having no talent. Don't believe his lies anymore. You are creative.

The world has beaten up some of us to the point we fear the power of chaos more than believe in the power of God. Remember how wolves defeat their prey? We can become so intimidated by chaos that we get stuck. We listen to every news alert and worry about every turn of events. We end up spending more time with chaos than with God. The solution is to focus on the Father and what he is up to.

Eyes on God, not the chaos.

God doesn't underestimate our gifting. He infused us with gifts customized for who we are. He knows our potential. The enemy doesn't underestimate us either. He is well aware of the power that comes when we co-create with the Creator. And he fears it.

In *Wild at Heart,*[2] John Eldredge says:

> Do you know why there's been such an assault? The Enemy fears you. You are dangerous big-time. If you ever really got your heart back, lived from it with courage, you would be a huge problem to him. You would do a lot of damage . . . on the side of good. Remember how valiant and effective God has been in the history of the world? You are a stem of that victorious stalk.

I hope you're beginning to sense how God views your creativity. It is his interpretation we're after. Our creativity carries immense power. That's why it faces extreme opposition. There is an enemy set against your creativity, but that's no reason to be hesitant. Chaos comes at us with intention. We must have an even greater intention to overcome it.

But good intention alone isn't enough. Initiation is required.

---

2. *Wild at Heart*, by John Eldredge, Thomas Nelson Publishers.

The world has beaten up
some of us to the point we fear
the power of chaos more than
believe in the power of God.

I hope you're beginning to sense
how God views your creativity.
It is his interpretation we're after.

Fight Bravely and Die Quickly

In the movie *The Mask of Zorro,* a young fighter has lost much. He is angry and seeking revenge against the enemy. An older, wiser warrior—the sage—stops him from entering the battle unprepared.

"You would have fought very bravely and died very quickly," he says.

That's a sobering dose of reality. In our own strength, we could rush the field rather than adequately prepare, quickly exceeding our area of gifting and authority. We would fight bravely and die quickly.

If you're prone to charge into battle quickly, I hope this section slows you down. Especially those of you who know what you were born to do. You've been honing your skills for a while now. Perhaps you've received some level of acclaim. The more you understand what's really going on, the more you're ready to get off the bench and into the game.

Yet those who know their talents best can begin to rely on their gifts to get through whatever they face. Past success causes them to spend less time preparing for what's next. This is a real danger. Over time, that can lead an overconfidence in one's own strength. It's more of a fire, ready, aim approach.

It's great you want to do more. But doing comes after

being. When we are overconfident, we tend to rely on our power and talent more than on preparation and discipline to master what God has given us. We are not called to do things *for* God unless we're first willing to do those things *with* God. To be the student rather than the master.

Before inviting you into something larger, God wants to initiate you.

Because, let's face it: as talented as you are, you've been slammed pretty hard by chaos. Or perhaps you're weary from trying to do everything in your own strength. What you need for this part of the journey is an extra dose of patience and humility. Be open to learning a new way to pursue what you love to do. Be willing to be the student rather than the expert. Don't assume you already know your role in the story that hasn't been told yet.

Our goal isn't to go fast or to go slow, but to go at God's pace. It's good to remember that God is always on time but never in a hurry.

Gaining wisdom and training for our specific gifting is essential. We must learn how and where to wield our weapons to fight for beauty, light, and order. The hour is growing late. The interests we've been given aren't simply for our own enjoyment or profit. It's not a time to amuse ourselves by endlessly throwing paint against the wall to see what sticks.

Our creativity isn't just for—or about—us. Not in such a time as this.

We are not called to do things
for God unless we're first
willing to do those things *with* God.
To be the student rather
than the master.

Don't assume you already
know your role in the story
that hasn't been told yet.

A Paintbrush to Stop a Hurricane

In the face of such massive havoc, our talents may seem inconsequential. A nice gesture but far too little. Like holding up a paintbrush to ward off an oncoming hurricane.

But when millions enter into their God-given creativity in their realms of authority and boldly use it for good, chaos trembles.

I imagine it's a bit like Joshua and his warriors must have felt when God told them his strategy for defeating Jericho. Allow me to paraphrase the story from Joshua 6.

"Okay, here's our strategy. We're going to circle the impenetrable gate around the entire city. Armed men will lead the procession. But we won't be using those weapons. They'll be followed by seven priests blowing trumpets made from ram's horns. Keep your eyes on these guys. Behind them, more priests will carry the Ark of the Covenant, followed by more guards."

A warrior raises his hand. "Um, what happens then?"

"Nothing. And we'll do exactly the same for five more days. And nothing will happen those days either. But on the seventh day we'll all march around the city not once but six times. And on the seventh pass, the priests will give one long, loud trumpet blast and everyone will shout. Then the walls will come down. Any questions?"

That sure doesn't sound like a winning military strategy. Or a very intimidating show of power against a massively armed, walled, and legendary city. Yet, God used trumpet-playing priests to usher in the crumbling walls. It was a wild, miraculous victory.

I'm sure no one was more astonished than they were.

I feel a bit like I'm holding one of those trumpets now as I share this message with you. Or maybe a paintbrush in the face of massive chaos. I know the invitation feels so counterintuitive. How could our creativity—our writings, teaching, singing, sculpting, business skills—possibly play a major role in God's plans to defeat the chaos around us?

But consider this: From the beginning, the enemy has tried to use chaos against the Creator and creation. Today, he also opposes us and our creativity. I'm convinced chaos is fueled by the enemy's intense hatred for all who are trying to bring life and light into the world.

If you have recently been tempted to walk away from your gifting or put it on hold until things calm down—don't. Who you are and your unique talents are bringing much needed warmth and light into a world that grows colder and darker by the day.

Chaos is coming against your creativity because it knows that creativity can effectively come against it. In other words, it is making a preemptive strike, similar to what might have happened if a force had tried to silence the priest's trumpets before their seventh day victory march.

I believe its ultimate goal is to take us out before we can take it out. Making you more chaotic is just phase one. An advance attack to decrease the odds of you ever stepping into all God intends for your life.

Whether it's a paintbrush or a trumpet, when we embrace the gifting God's given us, it can stop a hurricane or cause a wall to tumble.

Let's discover what that looks like for you.

Whether it's a paintbrush
or a trumpet,
when we embrace
the gifting God's given us,
it can stop a hurricane or
cause a wall to tumble.

What Makes Your Heart Beat Faster?

If you're a bit puzzled by what pursuing your creativity looks like, that's normal.

The discovery process is finding out what makes us come alive. It's knowing what you love to do—which isn't always the same as what you're paid to do or even as what comes naturally. You may be amazing at a skill that brings you no joy. It pays the bills but doesn't bring life. I'm not saying you should stop doing that. I'm suggesting you also start discovering what makes your heart beat faster.

Surprisingly, I've found this is actually hardest for those who are good enough at numerous pursuits. The problem is they aren't sure where to focus. So they do a lot of things pretty well but never slow down to go deep and fully master any one thing.

The invitation is to exploration. Spend time thinking of what made you come alive as a young child. What happened to that desire? Did you set it aside for the more practical aspects of life? Or did it get diminished or attacked by the enemy enough times that you just gave up on it? Spend time remembering . . . and learning to dream again.

Even more important, invite God into the process. He'd love to stir and awaken the longings he placed in you before time began. Understand why God designed you to be creative in the unique ways you are. Then align your motive for why you create with his motive for making you, you. This relates to the trueness of who you are and how you create. We'll explore that more a bit later.

But the goal here isn't *just* to know more about your creativity. That pursuit keeps the focus on us. The journey to deeper, more authentic creativity—the kind that has an eternal spark—never starts or stays there.

True creativity begins with the Creator. Desire to know him. To spend time together, on walks, in conversation. Ask him questions. Share your dreams and disappointments. Read Scripture. Soak up worship music. Spend time in movies and books that draw you closer to him. I promise you this: the more you pursue God, the more you will find him in new and unexpected and playful ways.

How could that experience not change your art? How could it not change you?

And for all of you wanting a practical exercise, this next part of our journey is for you. Just ahead is an empty auditorium. I'll meet you there.

The discovery process is finding out what makes us come alive. It's knowing what you love to do—which isn't always the same as what you're paid to do or even as what comes naturally.

If our art just points back to us,
we're shining the light in
the wrong direction.

The Empty Auditorium

Welcome to what I call the Empty Auditorium experiment.

Imagine you're in a room designed for an audience. Maybe it seats ten. Maybe ten thousand.

How big is the room? You decide. But remember, this isn't a solo activity. God is with you. So ask for his wisdom.

Now go ahead and sit down in the middle of the stage. Take in the room. You can fill it with whomever you want. Who would it be? The young? The experienced? Believers? Skeptics? Families? Singles? The unseen? The powerful?

Another way to ask this is, who are the ones hungry for what you love to offer?

The only invalid answer is, "I'd fill it with everyone." That's a nonanswer. It keeps the focus vague and thus meaningless. So aim for a specific audience. Then, if you like, add a secondary audience. For instance, you might say the main group you hope to reach is young families. But that grandparents are a secondary audience because though they no longer have young kids, they do help with them.

Now that you have your ideal audience, what do you want to pour into them? Notice I didn't ask how they could make you feel important or good about yourself.

You are there for them. They are coming to have some need met or desire fulfilled.

Our gifting is this awkward mix of the personal and sacrificial. Creating something begins with pursuing what brings us life. But for our creativity to be more than a vanity project, it must address a felt need or point of pain in those who encounter us and our art. If our art just points back to us, we're shining the light in the wrong direction.

Though it's from us, our art at some point becomes no longer about us.

We elevate our art by remembering who infused us with our skills and who we are making it for. We drag it down by expecting it to elevate us.

So what would you build or say or teach or sing? What would you create for those in your auditorium? What help would you offer? And how would your creativity make the world a better place?

Don't let the endless possibilities overwhelm you. As you imagine creativity, don't see it as a once-in-a-lifetime opportunity. That just adds pressure. Rather, see it as the passion you have for this season of life. It what makes your heart beat faster . . . for now.

The Empty Auditorium experiment is powerful because—to use our earlier language—it is you entering into a void and empty space to bring beauty, life, order, and hope through who you are and what you do.

Your primary identity is
a son or daughter of God.
The world didn't give you
that identity and it can't
take it from you.

Good mechanics don't define
a car by its current state.
They test what's broken
to restore it.
Likewise, personality tests
don't define us but reveal
our current state and how
we try to make life work.

But If You Knew Me

We can limit our creative potential by limiting how we see ourselves.

As we've already discussed, your primary identity is a son or daughter of God. The world didn't give you that identity and it can't take it from you.

But from there, further definitions can become unhelpful. The more descriptors we add, the less we become.

We take on the label of the make-it-happen person. Or the person who is great behind the scenes. We name ourselves as passive. Or aggressive. But are these labels true? Even if you like what they say about you?

Let me ask you a question. Are you introverted or extroverted? Before you answer (and I know you already have an answer), let me ask a few more questions.

Is Jesus an introvert or extrovert? How about God?

I'm guessing those questions gave you pause. Me too. Because, well, the tests are incapable of defining God and Jesus.

Jesus savored time alone. And Jesus was also fully himself with large groups of people. God is wholly content in his own presence. And he created a world that works best when people learn how to love him and love others. By design, it's a messy, unpredictable way for our stories to unfold. Likely not the system an introvert would create.

God made us in his image. Jesus invites us to become more like him. But will doing so make us more introverted or more extroverted?

What I'm getting at is that something greater is at play.

And definitions can be more limiting than true.

Personality tests measure the status quo but can't predict the new creation God is inviting you to be. The real test is who you're becoming, not who you were yesterday. If a test measures your brokenness rather than your true self, the worst thing to do is tattoo those test results on your arm or your heart and believe *this* is who you are.

Good mechanics don't define a car by its current state. They test what's broken to restore it. Likewise, personality tests don't define us but reveal our current state and how we try to make life work.

Ask God who he made you to be. Your true identity is God given, not test-driven. Rather than letting personality tests limit our potential, let's recognize the limits of these tests as well as the effects of chaos, which try to make us forget who we are or to act as we're not.

I can hear the doubt slipping away. But some of you feel stuck. "If you only knew me . . ."

I don't. But God does. He created you and knows everything about you.

Let him keep shaping you into the you he had in mind from before time began. This is the way to freedom.

How to Make Anything

In the book of Exodus, we're given a glimpse into how God infuses people with creativity.

Have you ever heard of Bezalel? His name isn't likely to make the short list of best baby names. But perhaps it should. The name means "in the protection or shadow of God."

Moses wrote that God called Bezalel, who was of the tribe of Judah, *by name* and then *filled him with the Spirit of God* in wisdom, understanding, knowledge, and in all craftsmanship.

Let that sink in. God called him by name. He extended a personal invitation: "Hey, Bezalel. I have a big project for you. It will stretch your creativity in ways you can't imagine."

You can imagine things quickly shifted from intimate to intimidating for Bezalel. Because the invitation was for something beyond him. The invitation required initiation.

It was beyond him. But not up to him. God then filled him with the Spirit of God in wisdom, understanding, knowledge, and in all craftsmanship. God gives him mission impossible and then makes it possible. It isn't about Bezalel coming through while God watches with his arms crossed. It is the Creator inviting and empowered us to co-create with him.

> The person who lives in right relationship with God does it by embracing what God arranges for him. Doing things for God is the opposite of entering into what God does for you.
> (Galatians 3:11–12 MSG)

What did God call Bezalel to do? God assigned Bezalel with the honor of being the chief architect and artisan of the tabernacle. His responsibilities included—but weren't limited to—overseeing the creation of the Ark of the Covenant, the priestly garments, wood and stone carvings, metal work, and the holy oils. Beyond these skilled crafts, he was also to be a skilled teacher.

> Moses told the Israelites, "See, God has selected Bezalel son of Uri, son of Hur, of the tribe of Judah. He's filled him with the Spirit of God, with skill, ability, and know-how for making all sorts of things, to design and work in gold, silver, and bronze; to carve stones and set them; to carve wood, working in every kind of skilled craft. And he's also made him a teacher, he and Oholiab son of Ahisamach, of the tribe of Dan. He's gifted them with the know-how needed for carving, designing, weaving, and embroidering in blue, purple, and scarlet fabrics, and in fine linen. They can make anything and design anything." (Exodus 35:30–35 MSG)

God filled Bezalel and his students with his Spirit. Then they could "make *anything* and design *anything*." Not in their strength. Not due to their amazingness. It was only possible *with* God's filling.

I hope this encourages you. God has called you by name. He's infused you with a specific set of skills and gifts. And now he's filling you with skill and ability to affect the atmosphere around you. The pressure is off to come through or be amazing.

Simply pursue what you love with God and ask him to fill you with his Spirit. Yes, learn your craft. Put in the hours. Do the work. But start from a foundation of intimacy and humility. What God has given you to do is beyond you, for you, and never up to you.

Learn to pursue your

creativity with God.

You will discover why it matters.

Why the enemy opposes it.

And just how powerful

God-given creativity can be.

The Master's Wheel

It is time we return to *The Mask of Zorro* movie.

What happens after the experienced sage saves the young Zorro from certain death by holding him back from a fight he isn't prepared to win?

The brash young man angrily pushes back, saying he could have won the fight. But he was untrained. He would have fought bravely and died quickly.

The wise warrior is after more. He's been Zorro before.

He sees potential. He knows how the young Zorro has much promise. But victory is only possible by choosing humble mastery over immediate action.

"You know," the older Zorro remarks, "there is a saying, a very old saying: when the pupil is ready the master will appear."

Only with the younger Zorro's consent does the sage begin training him for future victory. It begins by the sage placing him in a large circle on a stone floor. The older Zorro announces, "This is called a training circle. The Master's Wheel. This circle will be your world. Your whole life. Until I tell you otherwise, there is nothing outside of it."

That you have made it this far on our journey reveals your desire for more. Now it your time to step into the Master's Wheel.

The training circle is where you will learn to pursue your creativity with God. You will discover why it matters. Why the enemy opposes it. And just how powerful

God-given creativity can be.

I'll offer you what God has shown me while being well aware that I'm still a student. Maybe I'm a bit farther on this journey than you. Or perhaps you're well beyond me and this is simply a refresher.

Either way, we're all students learning from the true Master.

> Now God has us where he wants us, with all the time in this world and the next to shower grace and kindness upon us in Christ Jesus. Saving is all his idea, and all his work. All we do is trust him enough to let him do it. It's God's gift from start to finish! We don't play the major role. If we did, we'd probably go around bragging that we'd done the whole thing! No, we neither make nor save ourselves. God does both the making and saving. He creates each of us by Christ Jesus to join him in the work he does, the good work he has gotten ready for us to do, work we had better be doing. (Ephesians 2:9–10 MSG)

Before we step into the circle and discover more about our powers and how to wield them, I need to reveal some key distinctions of our Master's Wheel.

Your canvas is the place where your presence and gifting play out.

What is done in union with God

has the power to transcend us

and ripple far beyond

this moment in time.

Your Canvas

Your canvas is the place where your presence and gifting play out.

But before your creativity can happen on the canvas, a transformation must happen in you. And that process requires training.

It's time to join the young Zorro in mastering the circle. Time to join Katniss Everdeen in surviving the ultimate games. Time to train with underdog Rocky Balboa in the boxing ring. Each was becoming something more than they were. Their future victories would first be won in the hidden places.

We each have our scars from encounters with chaos. Though we've fought bravely in the only ways we knew, we've been beaten.

But there is another way. We can overcome what comes against us if we will train for it.

Through training, we will learn to use our creativity with God to bring light and order and hope into this empty world and to transform whatever chaos we can within our realm of authority.

Through practice, we will discover the power of trying new things, asking big questions, and testing our limits. We will realize what it means to truly pursue our creativity with God in a way that lights the darkness.

And with the help of other sages and fellow travelers, we will see that we are not alone. God will introduce you to kindred spirits in the most unexpected ways. You will sense God's presence like never before. You will understand your limits, yet see God surpass them through creative fellowship with him and others.

You will see your spark grow into a flame. And you will be in awe to see the unexpected ways it spreads. Not just from what you do, but as that combines with the efforts of countless others discovering how to infuse an eternal spark into their homes, neighborhoods, and communities.

That is the fellowship you are being invited into. You are not alone.

But it is why your dreams and creativity have been so opposed.

The enemy knows creativity with an eternal spark is a doorway to intimacy with the Father and to the restoration of what has been lost and stolen. What is done in union with God has the power to transcend us and ripple far beyond this moment in time. Of course, the enemy will throw every bit of chaos he can at us. He wants to disconnect you from God and derail your efforts by filling you with fear and nothingness.

Though God's ultimate victory is assured, our daily battles are intense. We aren't given an advance warning of every coming storm. Tragedy often strikes in the blink of an eye. That's why we must train now. We can only counter the forces of chaos by being firmly rooted in the One who has overcome the world and every form of chaos within it.

Our Master's Wheel will work differently than Zorro's in a few key ways, primarily in the direction we're moving. The young Zorro's training began in the larger, outer circles. As his skill increased, he progressed to a smaller circle. With each victory, his world contracted until he made it to the center.

But his ultimate goal was revenge. Ours is love.

Zorro had a sage guiding him through the Master's Wheel. We have the Master.

So we begin instead at the center, discovering the foundational power of starting with God. Then we will pursue changes in us before we seek to change the chaos around us. Each victory will take us farther out. As we align more with God in our presence and gifting, our world doesn't contract, it expands. As do we. By the time we are at the final outer ring, we will be a new person.

Our Master's Wheel has eleven circles. Picture each level as a concentric circle. We'll begin in the center and move outward, one circle at a time. Heads-up: some levels will be easy; others will require more effort. The degree of difficulty varies by person and by where you are in this season. So be patient. Transformation takes time.

After starting his journey, the young Zorro asked impatiently, "What is lesson number 3?" The older Zorro responded, "To get to lesson 4."

The goal isn't to get somewhere first or fast. It's to arrive at the next level more fully you.

As we align more with God
in our presence and gifting,
our world doesn't contract,
it expands.

The Center: With

Knowing your creative gifts is important. Knowing God is far more so. Intimacy *with* God always comes before impact *for* God.

That's why we must begin here.

God knit your gifts into you before you were born. He gave you specific passions so the two of you could pursue them together. The more you do, the more you know God. The more you know God, the more you discover your true identity and purpose. This is a beautiful never-ending circle.

But "doing" isn't the most important thing to God. He created Adam and Eve and loved them fully before they did anything.

At the start of this quest, I asked God for wisdom. Part of that decision was rooted in the promise that God would be a sage for me on this journey.

> Call to me and I will answer you. I'll tell you marvelous and wondrous things that you could never figure out on your own. (Jeremiah 33:3 MSG)

Remember, we can only experience these things *with* God. He makes it clear we won't see or hear them in our own strength or apart from his presence.

Imagine God invited you on a road trip. He knows a

secret route that no one else travels. If you go, he will be your personal tour guide. He'll show you new colors and discuss never-before-thought-of ideas. You'll need a new language to describe what you see.

But let's say you decline the offer. After all, your calendar is full. Besides, you prefer not to go anywhere without knowing all the details in advance. And, come on, you're confident that you could get there on your own anyway.

God always gives you that choice. No matter the situation, you can either call out to God, who will show you infinite possibilities, or you can pursue the finite options you see with your limited vision and strength.

It's freeing to realize not everything is up to you. As I say in my book *The Story of With*: "God doesn't need your help as much as he wants your heart. Whenever you start to focus more on your talents and gifts than on him, you miss the main invitation. Which is to pursue them together. With him."

This version of "with" can feel disruptive, inconvenient, and inefficient as you allow God to set the rhythm of your day. You look to God to know when your work is done. You seek God, not the world, for validation. You pursue God, not past formulas, for new ideas. Productivity is good. God's presence, however, is the foundation. Everything else, including *all* external metrics of success, are secondary.

When Moses was tasked with leading the people out of the desert, he made this bold statement to God:

> Moses said, "If your presence doesn't take the lead here, call this trip off right now. How else will it be known that you're with me in this, with

me and your people? Are you traveling with us or not?" (Exodus 33:15–16 MSG).

When was the last time you said those words to God about a project you were working on?

When your story, the one you're living, feels stuck, that's the perfect time to call out to God. He will answer. Let him know you refuse to move forward without his active, intimate presence. Invite him to show you marvelous things and remarkable options you'd never know on your own.

Doing so will infuse your heart—and your art—with an eternal spark that no conference or consultant can ever duplicate. God loves making the previously impossible possible.

As hard as it may be to believe, God's desire is to spend time co-creating with you rather than nodding in approval at a finished work that you did alone.

If you want your art to have an eternal spark, God has to breathe life into your creativity, not just you. That is creative fellowship.

What are some basic ways to begin co-creating with God?

- Begin with expectancy. Ask God what he has planned for your time together.
- Invite God to infuse your creativity beyond your imagination (Jeremiah 33:3).
- Follow God's lead. If he takes you on what seems like a detour, go there.
- Like Moses, be willing to call off the endeavor if you don't sense God's presence.

- Ask God what he thinks of your creativity. Rest in his validation.
- When done each day, give what was accomplished back to God as an offering.

The goal isn't to create something *for* God. It is to create something *with* God.

That's why we must begin here. If we approach our training circle from the inverse order, we pursue life in our own strength and then hope God is somehow in it. But that approach never works. When we finally get to the center of that circle, we find it hollow.

That's because God will not be last. He must be first. He is the center.

Intimacy with God always comes
before impact for God.

God's desire is to spend time co-creating with you rather than nodding in approval at a finished work that you did alone.

Level 10: Transformation

Before we can even consider changing the chaos around us, God must first transform the chaos within us.

Our creativity can't be transformed until we are.

Who we are comes before what we do. Right being is what determines the right doing. Never the opposite. Which is why our presence is more powerful than our gifting. We can do what we do only because of who we are. This is why chaos tries to make us forget who we are . . . and to become more like it.

With God, you can create in the empty places by reshaping (*Tohu*) and filling the void with light (*Vohu*).

But before that can happen, God must reshape and fill the void places within you. This is part of his process of making us a new creation (2 Corinthians 5:17). Pursue this before you focus on what you are creating.

As the old things pass, you will become more like Jesus. And the impact will be stunning.

How might this look?

Sometimes our most creative act is simply to walk into a room and change the atmosphere through our presence with a smile. A hug. Eye contact with a person who feels unseen. Listening to another's story. A shared meal. Often we don't have to say a word.

There are endless ways to bring light into the darkness.

Our presence is more powerful
than our gifting.
We can do what we do only
because of who we are.
This is why chaos tries to
make us forget who we are
. . . and to become more like it.

Level 9: Co-Creation

In this circle, we're going to explore the act of creating with God.

This is important because many unknowingly downgrade what is possible at the very point they seek to pursue their talents with God.

They miss the joy of co-creating because they believe that the best that can be attained is sub-creating. The distinction between co-creating and sub-creating is massive.

Co- means "with" and *sub-* means "under."

Sub-creation views the creative process somewhat like this: God is up in the sky, far above us. He's given us specific gifts and talents. Now he's waiting to see what we do with them. So we get busy and create things for God. Then we lift them up, hopeful that he approves. J. R. R. Tolkien's essay, "On Fairy Stories" presents his views on sub-creating. He's obviously a master storyteller, but I prefer God's invitation to co-create.

Creation is intimate act, not something God subcontracts out to us and then checks in occasionally to make sure we're doing our job right. There's oversight but no intimacy in that process.

Co-creation is more like a dance. God isn't up there somewhere. He is with us. Present. And we're on the playground of ideas together.

Does this concept of co-creation diminish God's authority? Absolutely not. There's no question he is the Creator and we are his creation. He is Father and we are sons and daughters. There's no contest. And there's nothing we have to earn or prove.

Imagine a father-daughter dance where the dad invites his daughter but then, once at the dance, he stands off to the side. He isn't there to dance but to evaluate how she dances. That would be tragic. The whole point is to dance together.

The magic happens when the young girl puts her feet on top of her father's shoes and he leads. He savors the interaction, the playfulness, the joy. But what if, as the song ends, the young girl rushes back to her friends and says, "Did you see me dancing? Wasn't it amazing?" And the father interrupts, "It wasn't your dance. I drove us here. I bought your dress. I led us every moment of the dance. Never forget, I'm the alpha here."

Do you see how toxic that view is?

Compare that to the shared experience of a good father and daughter dancing together. Yes, the dad set things in motion. He's in charge. Yet in his authority, he invites her to join him. And from that moment forward, it is a shared experience.

God does the same with us. He invites us to enter into our gifting actively and intimately with him. He's not up there. He's right here, with us.

We ask God for a plan—because information is our goal. God invites us into a dance—because intimacy is his goal.

When we keep God at a distance because we feel that is more reverent or respectful, we miss the dance of creation. As a good friend of mine says, "God is the least religious person I know." God invites us into relationship, not religion. Relationship is intimate, not distant. God created us to do life together with him. He would love to co-create with you.

The music is starting. God is waiting for you on the dance floor. Will you join him?

We ask God for a plan—

because information is our goal.

God invites us into a dance—

because intimacy is his goal.

Level 8: The Vine and the Void

This eighth circle requires much of us. And it exposes much.

It reveals whether we are attached to the Vine or the void.

Jesus says:

> Remain in me, as I also remain in you. No branch can bear fruit by itself; it must remain in the vine. Neither can you bear fruit unless you remain in me.
>
> I am the vine; you are the branches. If you remain in me and I in you, you will bear much fruit; apart from me you can do nothing. If you do not remain in me, you are like a branch that is thrown away and withers; such branches are picked up, thrown into the fire and burned. If you remain in me and my words remain in you, ask whatever you wish, and it will be done for you. (John 15:4–7 NIV)

If we remain connected to the Vine, we will accomplish great things (bear much fruit). But if we do not, we can do nothing. Not do pretty well. Not pull it together in our own strength.

Nothing.

Not only that, if we don't stay tethered to the Vine, we are like branches tossed into the fire and burned. In other words, by our choice we end up in chaos. Clearly, we want to stay connected to the Vine.

The void does everything to pull us from the Vine. To create doubt. Bring disappointment. Numb our hearts. Diminish our good desires. And steal the passion for our creativity. All of it, swallowed up by a big gaping hole of nothingness.

The Spirit opposes that. You'll recall in Genesis 1:2 how God's spirit hovered over the void and began transforming this vast emptiness into beauty, life, and order.

We have a choice when the void that is chaos tries to deplete our dreams and pull us into emptiness. We can stay connected to the Vine, allowing the Creator's creativity to flow through us. Or get sucked into the void.

The void is empty of ideas. That's why when we're there, we tend to rely on formula to see us through. There are no higher thoughts from God. So we look to what we've done before, hoping it will somehow work again.

The void lures us to formula. Detached from the Vine, we feel like it's the only way to get things done. Creation is about bringing something new into existence. Formula is about re-creating what has been through a repetitive series of steps. It seeks to gain similar results by duplicating what's worked in the past. That's great for a muffin mix. Not for your art.

But God didn't overcome chaos with formula. He overcame it with his creativity and his presence, neither of which is predictable or repetitive. God makes all things new—not all things the same.

> He who was seated on the throne said, "I am making everything new!" Then he said, "Write this down, for these words are trustworthy and true." (Revelation 21:5 NIV)

We have the same opportunities to transform the void and emptiness in other people's lives and in the world's raging turmoil.

The void is hollow at its core. The Vine provides life at his core.

Jesus is our Vine. He is also the Word through which everything was made (see John 1). Look at what God says about Jesus being the Word:

> So shall My word that goes from My mouth;
> It shall not return to Me void,
> But it shall accomplish what I please,
> And it shall prosper in the thing for which I sent it.
> (Isaiah 55:11 NKJV)

The Word (Jesus) goes into the void but never returns void. The Word changes the void. The Word accomplishes what God pleases. It completes its mission every time with 100 percent success.

Jesus is our Vine. When we stay attached to him, we can do the impossible. Because no longer are we limited by our limitations. We are connected to the One who knows no limits.

If we remain connected to the Vine, we will accomplish great things (bear much fruit). But if we do not, we can do nothing. Not do pretty well. Not pull it together in our own strength.

Nothing.

Level 7: Heart

No great art was ever created without great heart.

No great life was ever lived without great heart.

Perhaps that's why God tells us the heart is central to all we are and do.

> Above all else, guard your heart,
> for everything you do flows from it.
> (Proverbs 4:23 NIV)

Everything you do flows from it.

Some teach that the heart is deceptive above all things (Jeremiah 17:9). They quit reading before hearing the rest of the story. That's tragic. Because God also said:

> I will give you a new heart and put a new spirit in you; I will remove from you your heart of stone and give you a heart of flesh. (Ezekiel 36:26 NIV)

Imagine what kind of new art you could create from a new heart. It's exciting to consider. Jesus understands the foundational importance of the heart. He defined his earthly mission by quoting this Scripture from Isaiah:

> He has sent Me to heal the brokenhearted,
> To proclaim liberty to the captives. (Isaiah 61:1 NKJV)

That's a big thought. Take a moment to let that sink in. Jesus defined his mission as healing our hearts and setting us free.

How free would you say you are? What is the condition of your heart? Nothing matters more…so take time at this level to examine how you are doing in this key area.

The Spirit gives us the ability to keep chaos out of our hearts while filling it instead with the fruit of the Spirit.

> But the Holy Spirit produces this kind of fruit in our lives: love, joy, peace, patience, kindness, goodness, faithfulness, gentleness, and self-control. (Galatians 5:22–23 NLT)

And it gets even better. When you align your heart with God, he promises to give you the desires of your heart.

> Take delight in the Lord,
> and he will give you the desires of your heart.
> (Psalm 37:4 NIV)

This means that we no longer have to wait for external circumstances to change or become calm. The calm is already within us.

Beyond that, we don't have to strive for the things we desire. God will give them to us. If we start with him.

Having a heart that's fully alive changes everything. That's the secret to this circle.

Creation is about bringing
something new into existence.
Formula is about re-creating
what has been through
a repetitive series of steps.
It seeks to gain similar results
by duplicating what's worked
in the past.
That's great for a muffin mix.
Not for your art.

We no longer have to wait
for external circumstances
to change or become calm.
The calm is already within us.

Level 6: Recovery

The previous levels have set our trajectory with a foundation based on unity with God and the essential importance of our heart.

We now have the grounding to see what's really going on.

This circle is what I refer to as a "situational awareness level." It shifts us from being reactive to proactive.

Let's begin with an observation: the more chaotic life becomes, the less creative we are. At least until we understand what's really going on and take action.

It seems like our gifting is being stolen from us . . . because it is.

But here's the reality check. Does this loss sound significant or like something of low importance in the midst of a raging storm? I mean, when everything is going wrong, should our creativity *really* make the top-ten list of what matters? At a time when chaos makes its presence known in every area of our lives, is a decreased creative desire a big deal? Should we just set those dreams aside until things calm back down?

No. Never.

Our creativity is immensely important. The loss of it during chaotic times isn't an unintended or ancillary consequence. It is a major target. We have an enemy who seeks to steal, kill, and destroy (John 10:10). And a skilled thief never sets out to steal something of no value.

The enemy is trying to steal your creative gifting. Because it is of great value.

The war against the Creator and creation that has been going on since before the beginning is still in motion, and your creativity has a role to play in winning the war. That is why you are being targeted and the enemy wants to throw chaos at your creativity. Don't underestimate its value.

At a time when chaos makes
its presence known in every area of
our lives, is a decreased
creative desire a big deal?
Should we just set those dreams
aside until things calm back down?

No. Never.

We have an enemy who seeks to
steal, kill, and destroy (John 10:10).
And a skilled thief never sets out
to steal something of no value.

Level 5: Fuel

Each day, we awake empty and fill ourselves anew. The choice is yours—to be filled with God or become more full of yourself.

What we choose for fuel matters.

If you're training for a marathon, it's not a good idea to fill yourself with a dozen hamburgers and fries each day. If you're taking a cross-country road trip you wouldn't fill your gas tank with molasses.

It's an even worse idea to fill yourself with the wrong things. We need to be intentional about everything we let in.

Yet where we usually let our guard down is with entertainment. We decide to see a new movie based on who's in it or who directed it, then tolerate whatever comes next. We sing a song because we love the catchy beat. Yet the words coming out of our mouths are about things we'd never normally agree with.

We open our minds, allow the toxins in, and then wonder why we have less hunger for God and more for the junk food of this world.

The creators of these works may say they are just reflecting life as they see it. And that may be an honest answer. Life without God is empty and void. Fear does seem more real than love. There really isn't much hope or reason to live other than pleasure. Their art is simply a mirror of their worldview.

They've let chaos in and are creating outwardly impressive but ultimately empty art. The problem is, empty isn't the same as harmless. We can't forget that when we consume art, we are letting the creator's worldview into our minds and hearts. It will have an impact on us. Everything we allow inside is either based in love or fear. Nothing is neutral.

Without the Creator, any creative work falls exponentially short of what it could have been. Our creations can't transcend us. There is no eternal spark because it was done without God. If you want to co-create with God, you have to choose the kind of creations that God wants to be involved in. If you don't, you're on your own.

And, as Jesus says, without me you can do nothing (John 15:5). No thing.

Jesus offers to fill us with living water.

> Jesus stood and said in a loud voice, "Let anyone who is thirsty come to me and drink. Whoever believes in me, as Scripture has said, rivers of living water will flow from within them."
> (John 7:37–38 NIV)

But the offer doesn't stop there. He desires to fill the entire universe with his goodness and trueness.

> Christ . . . ascended higher than all the heavens so that he might fill the universe with himself. (Ephesians 4:9–10 NLT)

What we fill ourselves with matters immensely. What we consume influences what we create:

> You'll do best by filling your minds and meditating on things true, noble, reputable, authentic, compelling, gracious—the best, not the worst; the beautiful, not the ugly; things to praise, not things to curse. (Philippians 4:8 MSG)

That's not a list of sanitized, safe, boring creations. Rather, it's confirmation that there are two ways to fill our minds. One leads to life and light. One leads to darkness and death.

What are we to do with the nothingness and emptiness around us? Fill it. Just like Elena filled the snow globes with living water.

But it starts with what you fill yourself with.

Each day, we awake empty
and fill ourselves anew.
The choice is yours—
to be filled with God or
become more full of yourself.

Level 4: True

Your creativity can take a million different forms.

But if it reflects the Creator, it will be true. Because God is true.

There is great freedom in pursuing your creativity in this manner, because it shifts the focus from manmade rules to creating like the Creator. God didn't create Christian mountains or oceans or elephants. He created each of these in trueness. Do the same.

True doesn't mean you should only create what can be proven.

Let your imagination usher in the new and not yet. But make sure those unheard notes and unseen realities align with how God made life. Let there be a great battle between good and evil. Let it be messy. Let it be real and raw. Or fantastical. But in whatever you create, let good and hope ultimately prevail. Not because that is nice and sweet, but because that is true. It's how God created the story we all find ourselves in.

Your creations also need to be true to who you are. The goal is never to create more like someone else. Don't try to be like ______________ (fill in the blank). We already have that person's flavor, color, voice, look. It was original when it was originated, not when it's repeated.

Your art will look different from everyone else's art.

And that's as it should be. God created mountains, sea otters, oceans, and oak trees. None remotely the same. All unique and all essential to creation. Bring your original ideas to the world. That's what we don't have yet. That's what we need.

Let your art blaze with God's trueness and your unique signature. Then invite us there.

God didn’t create Christian
mountains or oceans or elephants.
He created each of these
in trueness.
Do the same.

What good is a new beginning

if we are determined

to stay the same?

Level 3: Order

God created with passion and joy and wild creativity. But remember, he did so with Lady Wisdom at his side. And with Jesus and the Holy Spirit. There was an order to creation.

> For God is not a God of disorder but of peace. (1 Corinthians 14:33 NLT)

God is a God of order.

Perhaps that's why creativity actually comes most alive when there is order rather than chaos. Madeline L'Engle, the author of *Walking on Water* and *A Wrinkle in Time* noted:

> A life lived in chaos in an impossibility for the artist. No matter how unstructured may seem the painter's garret in Paris or the poet's pad in Greenwich Village, the artist must have some kind of order or he will produce a very small body of work. To create a work of art, great or small, is work, hard work, and work requires discipline and order.

In this circle, the focus is to invite wisdom and order into your creativity.

The only other option is chaos and disorder. Which is never a good idea.

It's important to note that order doesn't equate to comfort . . . or control. In this training circle, we must make peace with this uncomfortable truth. Giving birth to a new idea—especially one that counters the chaos in this world—is beautiful, messy, and costly. The goal is creation, not comfort. It Is to relinquish all illusion of control to God. And allow him to lead.

A friend of mine, Blaine Eldredge, puts it this way: "An artist's best work comes not from comfort but from the limitations and hard times of life."

The goal isn't a life of ease but to one of intention, purpose, and destiny. As L'Engle says, that path requires discipline and order. To walk it well, we must let go of control as we step into the unknown with God. Yes, there is tension in pursuing creativity in this way. It can feel inefficient and out of your control. That's good. Because control isn't the goal. But remember, control and order aren't the same substance. God is both the most creative being ever...and a God of order. He will be your sage every step of the way.

So ask yourself what you were born to bring into this world. Then decide how much you're willing to sacrifice in order to make it a reality. It will likely require discomfort and opposition. But if you are seeking to create something with an eternal spark, there is no other option.

Giving birth to a new idea—
especially one that counters
the chaos in this world—
is beautiful, messy, and costly.
The goal is creation, not comfort.

Think of your creativity as
a sword created with God's light.
This weapon is our presence and
our art fused together with God.
When wielded properly,
it pierces the darkness.
It overcomes fear with love.
It causes chaos to crumble.

Level 2: Weapons of Light

The first thing you notice about this level is the warm glow throughout it. In this circle, we will learn the immense power of God's light.

Light is the first thing God created on day one of creation. There was no sun. Just his light. And it was good. But his light isn't limited to the creation of this world.

God clothes himself in light:

> The Lord wraps himself in light as with a garment. (Psalm 104:2 NIV)

And in Revelation, the last book of the Bible, we are reminded again that our true source of light comes from God, not the sun.

> There will be no more night. They will not need the light of a lamp or the light of the sun, for the Lord God will give them light. (Revelation 22:5 NIV)

Imagine your creativity as a sword created with God's light. This weapon is our presence and our art fused together *with God*. When wielded properly, it pierces the darkness. It overcomes fear with love. It causes chaos to crumble.

Think back to Elena's snow globe. Though fear was trying to overtake her small island, the last snow globe was filled with living water that shimmered with sparkling light. It was a weapon of light used by a girl who believed in what was possible. I chose the name Elena because it is derived from Greek words that mean "bright shining light." We are invited to join God and be part of his plan for lighting this dark world. Elena is, interestingly, also the name of the older Zorro's daughter in the movie, *The Mask of Zorro*.

No two light swords are the same. Each has a unique color and shape, custom-fitted to the individual. Other swords feel awkward in our hands or hold no interest for us because those aren't the gifts we've been given authority to wield.

Art is a weapon of warfare against chaos. Certainly not the only weapon at our disposal. But one that has continually changed the world for good through creativity in story, song, architecture, medicine, teaching, culinary, dance, technology, farming, and science.

> I pray that the light of God will illuminate the eyes of your imagination, flooding you with light, until you experience the full revelation of the hope of his calling—that is, the wealth of God's glorious inheritances that he finds in us, his holy ones! (Ephesians 1:18 TPT)

In this training circle, we discover we can't fight darkness with darkness. It's never smart combat to try and defeat chaos with more chaos.

We fight darkness with light.

> For what do righteousness and wickedness have in common? Or what fellowship can light have with darkness? (2 Corinthians 6:14 NIV)

What are we to be doing in a world of darkness, emptiness, and chaos? In the book of Isaiah, God reveals more about the power we have when we walk in his light.

> God's Message,
> the God who created the cosmos, stretched out the skies,
> laid out the earth and all that grows from it,
> Who breathes life into earth's people,
> makes them alive with his own life:
> "I am God. I have called you to live right and well.
> I have taken responsibility for you, kept you safe.
> I have set you among my people to bind them to me,
> and provided you as a lighthouse to the nations,
> To make a start at bringing people into the open, into light:
> opening blind eyes,
> releasing prisoners from dungeons,
> emptying the dark prisons. (Isaiah 42:5–7 MSG)

A simple yet powerful prayer when starting a new project or facing the unknown is, "Let there be light. Your light, God, on this decision, this issue, this problem, this opportunity."

Yes. In all we create, let there be light.

In this training circle,
we discover we can't fight
darkness with darkness.
It's never smart combat to try and
defeat chaos with more chaos.

The Outer Level: Change

Not letting chaos in is an essential practice. But living in that way is only the beginning of what is possible. God offers us the ability to do far more. To change the external chaos around us.

Remember Mr. Miyagi's words to the karate kid? "First learn stand. Then learn fly. Nature's rule, Daniel-san, not mine."

We've learned to stand. Now here in the final circle, It's time to learn to fly.

Let's look back at my definition of creativity:

> *God-infused creativity is using our presence and our gifting to bring something new into existence in a way that changes people and the atmosphere for good.*

We've explored how to bring something new into existence using our God-infused creativity. Now it is time to consider how we can transform the atmosphere through our presence and gifting.

This is rarely easy and always costly.

That's why this is the final level of the Master's Circle. It requires a certain level of humility and maturity. It also builds on every previous level.

But before we go further, it's important to discuss the concept of operating in your realm of authority.

God hasn't given any of us limitless ability to change the atmosphere everywhere. We each are given a realm of influence and authority. Our homes. Our children. Our job. Our creativity.

When we walk with God in these areas, we can change our world for good. And as more and more people change their realm for good, more of the world changes for good.

But if you try to come against chaos in ways that God hasn't authorized or empowered you to do, you can get shredded. You can fight bravely and die quickly.

The atmosphere you are able to change is only in the areas of authority you've been given.

That is not limiting. It is focused. There are countless others who have authority in areas you don't. As they walk in their gifting and presence, they'll have remarkable results. There's more than enough for each of us to do in our own realms. You can make a tremendous difference if you are present and prepared.

What do you do from here. What is the best next step?

Make something beautiful.

What might this look like? When chaos tries to enter into your home through an explosive argument or bad financial or medical news, you don't let fear in your heart. And you pour out what is within you. You release the fruit of the Spirit into the atmosphere. Suddenly the room is filled with love, joy, peace, patience, kindness, goodness, faithfulness, gentleness, and self-control (Galatians 5:22–23). The very atmosphere is permeated with something eternal. And chaos blinks. It falters. It fades.

You write a novel. You paint the ocean. You give birth

to an opera or a flower shop or a daycare center. And the atmosphere changes for good. Hope is reborn. Beauty is revealed. Love is made real. Hearts are reawakened. Light overcomes the darkness.

What part of the atmosphere were you born to change? This will be accomplished through your presence and your gifting. As long as you do so with God.

It is time for you to step fully into who God meant you to be when he created you. The world needs your creativity and presence.

I'm reminded of the prophet Isaiah's commissioning scene. He sees God on his throne and is undone. He feels totally unworthy.

> Then one of the seraphim flew to me with a live coal in his hand, which he had taken with tongs from the altar. With it he touched my mouth and said, "See, this has touched your lips; your guilt is taken away and your sin atoned for."
>
> Then I heard the voice of the Lord saying, "Whom shall I send? And who will go for us?"
>
> And I said, "Here am I. Send me!" (Isaiah 6:6–8 NIV)

The world has grown cold. We need stories, songs, and art that warm our souls and light the way. And we need them from those who have spent time with the Creator.

The world will be difference because of our presence. The only question is how?

Who you are and what you do will fill a void. In a classroom. At a sporting event. In a garden. In a hospital. Through a book. With a song. With the right word.

Your presence and gifting will ignite sparks of change around the world in countless ways. Your creativity will combat the chaos and impact the empty places in this life. And the light will overcome the darkness. One victory, one life, one decision at a time.

It isn't just enough. It is more than enough. It is everything.

The atmosphere you are able
to change is only in the areas of
authority you've been given.

That is not limiting. It is focused.

What do you do from here.
What is the best next step?

Make something beautiful.

The Choice Is Yours

Here we stand. At the edge of the outer circle. And at the end of our quest.

Well done. I am so proud of you.

We began this journey with a desire to overcome what comes against us. I know I'm in a new place. No matter how shaken this world gets, I will—like King David—make this my declaration:

> I see that the LORD is always with me. I will not be shaken, for he is right beside me. (Acts 2:25 NLT)

And my hope is you will declare the same. After all, look how far you've come. Consider all that you now understand about chaos and the Creator. About what's really going on. And your role to play in it.

That is true success.

Though the world offers us all kinds of ways to measure success, it isn't best measured by external outcomes. Only God can offer validation of who you are and what you're doing. True success is based on whether we pursue our dreams, projects and people in our realm of influence *with* God.

When we do, we experience success in the moment rather than hoping to achieve it after the fact, based on the response of others. We create from a place of success rather than from hope of achieving success.

So take the pressure off yourself and your creativity to always come through. Your performance cannot tell you who you are. Only God can do that. And he does so through your life first. As I've long said, you can't tell a better story than the one you're living. And your creativity can't transcend your life with the Creator.

Rather than chase success, chase big ideas with God.

And know this: everything you are meant to accomplish will not happen in the here and now, but in the larger scope of eternity. That thought alone takes away so much pressure. What you don't accomplish, what has been thwarted here, isn't the final word in your story.

It's essential for us to remember that while chaos isn't eternal, we are.

As sons and daughters of God, our training as co-creators is both for now—*and* for eternity. Our creativity doesn't end when we pass from here to everlasting life. In the coming kingdom, we'll more fully realize our gifts. And we'll get to do so in much greater freedom.

Everything that's opposed you and your dreams here will be gone. You will be the truest version of you that God always meant. Your creativity will no longer bound by space, time, or other limitations.

Imagine what you'll be able to do with colors and sounds that this world has never seen, and with all eternity to pursue the things you were created to do. We give young children crayons before paint because they're still learning how to draw. In the same way, we create in a certain dimension now. Imagine what we will breathe into existence as eternal beings.

What we can only imagine in part here, we will one day step into in full.

> Now we see things imperfectly, like puzzling reflections in a mirror, but then we will see everything with perfect clarity. All that I know now is partial and incomplete, but then I will know everything completely, just as God now knows me completely. (1 Corinthians 13:12 NLT)

If pursuing your creativity in the new heaven and new earth isn't something you've given thought to, I encourage you to dream big here. This is simply the beginning.

When you start to see your creativity in this way, it takes the pressure off. Not everything has to happen now. The Creator of time will give you enough time for what he's stirred in you to create. Either in this world or the next. God is always wooing us, as C. S. Lewis famously wrote in *The Last Battle*,[3] to go "further up and further in!"

Now, I have one final invitation. It will only take a few minutes.

Remember "The Last Snow Globe"? I'd like you to reread this simple story. I think you'll see it with new eyes now, because you're a different person than you were when we started this journey.

Jesus was, of course, right. In this shaken word, we will have trouble. But he has overcome the world. Because of that, we can overcome what comes against us.

We don't have to let chaos in. We have living water within us, like the last snow globe. And like Elena, we can break it open and offer it in sacrificial ways to change the world.

God can do all things. Chaos can't.

---

3. *The Last Battle*, by C.S. Lewis, HarperCollins

So in all you do, remember that God has given you a choice.

> Today I have given you the choice between life and death, between blessings and curses. Now I call on heaven and earth to witness the choice you make. Oh, that you would choose life, so that you and your descendants might live!
> (Deuteronomy 30:19 NLT)

Rather than focus on the beast on this island, may you choose life, love, and God.

May you choose to be astonished.

Our creativity doesn’t end when we
pass from here to everlasting life.
In the coming kingdom,
we’ll more fully realize our gifts.
And we’ll get to do so
in much greater freedom.

This Book is Far Better Because of the Insights, Encouragement, Prayers, and Gifting of These Astonishing Creatives:

Kellye Arnold
Greyson Arnold
Hope Arnold
Chase Arnold
Nadine Brandes
Kristy Cambron
Ashley Clark
Lorie DeWorken
John Eldredge
Stasi Eldredge
Blaine Eldredge
Sara Hagerty
Bart Hansen
Erin Healy
Kristin Ingebretson
Gale Jones
Mandy Nelson
Bill Perry
Jeff Robinson
Holly Varni

There Is More

Pursuing life and creativity with God is beautifully disruptive and immensely freeing. It begins with knowing God as both Creator and Father...and ourselves as his sons and daughters.

If you're tired of trying to get things done in your own strength or make success happen by following yet another formula, that's good. Because there is a better way. One that will awaken your heart...and your art.

As a fellow traveler,
I hope you'll join me in that journey.

Bonus Excerpt of *The Story of With: A Better Way to Live, Love & Create*

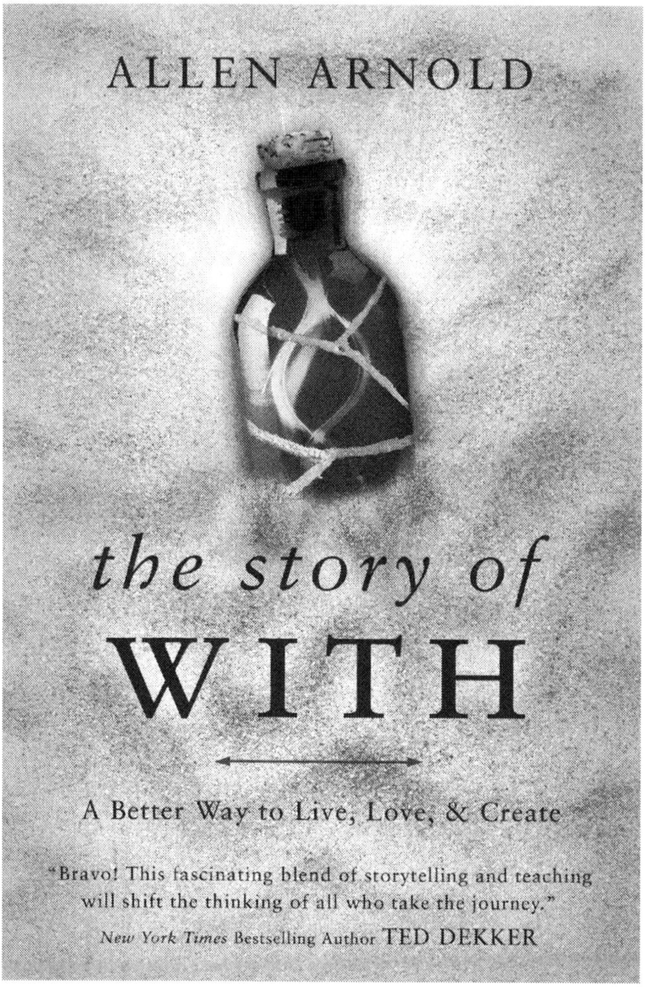

Paperback, Kindle, and Audible editions available at Amazon.com.

PART ONE

hunger *for* more

How The Fortune Cookie Crumbled

Most of us are stuck in a story of *without*. We go about our tasks and get through the day without much hope, without our dreams realized, without deep friendships, and without experiencing the presence of God.

> Most of us are stuck in a story of *without*.

For decades, I couldn't put words to how these missing pieces affected my life. But the result was a slow erosion of passion and a pull to what I felt I was able to control. If it were all up to me, then I would figure out the formula for the best possible life.

I was successful by the world's standards. Yet even in the moments when everything appeared good, an indescribable ache tugged at my soul. It was an emptiness that success couldn't satisfy coupled with a vague hope that there had to be more.

From the outside, I was on the fast track to the top. I began my career at some of the nation's most acclaimed advertising agencies. I later founded the fiction division at a top-ten publishing house. My role was to acquire talented storytellers and help bring their ideas to life. And it worked big time. I was recognized in a prestigious "40 under 40" publishing industry list as one of the top forty visionaries under age 40.

From a soul perspective, however, I was in a free fall to rock bottom.

I was an extremely driven man in search of a larger story. And then one day I thought I found the answer after a meal of Kung Pao chicken. Usually fortune cookies offer forgettable clichés, but not this time. The message inside this one put words to a worldview I resonated with: *"The one who says it can't be done should get out of the way of the one already doing it."*

It's not wise to take your life mantra from a fortune cookie, but I taped this one to my desk. More than that, I embraced it as truth. My worth would be in what I did. And I would be the one to make the impossible happen.

During my twenties and thirties, I felt I could open any door through sheer force of will. What seemed extreme to others was energizing to me. And the problem was, it was working.

Staring Down a Plane

What started as a normal workday quickly turned into a case of man versus plane. This event took place long before 9/11—at a time when airport security was far less than it is today. Otherwise, it may have been the last story of my life.

I was on a business call as I awaited my flight when I looked up to see the boarding area completely empty. I ran to the gate. "I have to get on that plane. I have an important meeting and my video crew is already on board."

"Your seat has been given to a standby passenger," the attendant said. "The plane has already left."

I looked through the large plate glass windows behind her at the runway. "Turn around and look," I pleaded. "The plane is right there. I've got to get on it."

"You're too late. You missed it," she said and walked away.

Where others would have conceded defeat, I was undeterred. I took a deep breath, pushed open the emergency exit door to the tarmac, and walked toward the runway as the alarm blared. I approached the small commuter plane, unsure what would happen next. I didn't have to wonder long. The pilot barged out of the plane, straight for me.

His bewilderment was no match for my singular determination to board the plane. Minutes later, the standby passenger was escorted off. The video crew couldn't believe what they had just witnessed. "Dude, you stared down a plane and it blinked first." I found the open seat and started reading a book, victorious and oblivious to the havoc I'd caused for everyone on the flight. Against the odds, I had made it happen. Now let's get this flight going.

I cringe at that story now. I was the bull in the china shop who relentlessly forced his way forward regardless of the cost. And there was always a cost—to my wife, my coworkers, and though unseen for years, my heart.

Several promotions later, I led a marketing team that initiated hundreds of national book campaigns. We were experiencing a season of immense success. One Friday, my boss invited me to what I thought was a casual lunch. Before taking the first bite of my sandwich, he began. "Allen, do you realize everyone on your team thinks you're a jerk?" His actual language was more colorful—and he was just getting started. "Not one of them enjoys being in your presence. They can't stand being around you. They only stay because you're good at what you do."

It was the last thing I expected, a sucker punch to the gut. Didn't he understand how challenging it was to keep these people in line? Wasn't he happy with the results? Sure, I was relentless with my expectations, but no more than I was on myself. I was the one who made things happen. And I was delivering success. Wasn't that what mattered?

I was delivering success. Wasn't that what mattered?

I stared at my boss, wanting to defend myself. Yet no words came. So I sat back and took it in. And in that moment, something in me shifted. I saw myself as others did, and I no longer wanted to be that man.

Chasing fast after the wrong definitions of success does accomplish one thing. It causes you to reach the end of yourself and the illusion of control sooner rather than later. I felt deep shame at who I was . . . but also a glimmer of hope in who I could become.

I believed God could make all things new . . . I just never realized it was me who needed to be made new. Though slowly at first, I began to see that God would father me if I simply allowed myself to be a son. I no longer had to have all the answers. My validation wasn't tied to the approval of others. My goal wasn't to get my to-do list completed, but simply to do whatever I did with God.

Over time, a fellowship of others came alongside me and helped me chart a better path. I would begin anew—no longer focused on building my own kingdom. Instead, as a restored King I would use whatever power I was given to care for those under my authority.

More than a decade later, I joined a ministry in Colorado. My supervisor welcomed me with these words: "Allen, we know you can get things done. But we want you for your presence—not your productivity." It was as if time stood still. I had come full circle from the conversation in the deli with my other boss. I had become a new man. And it all began with a disruptive invitation to *be* more, rather than *do* more.

Your Missing Super Powers

Maybe you've never been that driven. Perhaps you struggle with passivity. But can we agree something important has been lost? Even if you can't put your finger on it, there's a yearning inside, a sense that there has to be more.

I was recently waiting for a friend at a large gathering. Beside me was the Lost and Found bin. A woman walked up, peered in, and sorted through the various items. As she left empty-handed, she quipped, "Just seeing if my super powers were in there."

Exactly!

Something essential has gone missing. You've just been searching for it in the wrong place.

This is good news. It means you're not crazy for feeling that way. And it gets better. Because what's lost can be found—once you know where to look for it.

> Something essential has gone missing. You've just been searching for it in the wrong place.

What if this untapped strength we've lost track of is hidden in plain sight? What if the answer lies within our distinct desires, talents, and creativity? Could the God of all Creation have placed inside us, before we were even born, a homing device that ultimately would lead us back to Him? In other words, could the one thing we're most passionate about and skilled at doing also reveal the way to more life, love, and creativity?

That's not what the world teaches us. From childhood, it seems the message is that creativity is rare and reserved for the elite few. While it would be nice if everyone possessed a unique ability or talent, we're told that most folks didn't receive that secret sauce at birth.

But what if we did? What if *you* did?

For the moment, simply reorient yourself to this truth. You. Are. Creative.

It may not feel like it. You may not have experienced the reality of this yet. Or you may have been met with rejection when you share your unique talents with others.

But you are creative.

How could it be otherwise? Your bloodline traces back beyond your parents. The DNA of the Creator pulses through you. And the One who created sunsets, oceans, stars, and laughter cannot create something that doesn't have His eternal spark within it. He does not make generically creative beings. He wove into each of us a specific set of interests, passions, and curiosity—which holds clues to our greater destiny and our truer selves.

The answer isn't simply in discovering your creative gift. Many know and pursue their talents daily. If successful, it is how they are defined . . . or come to define themselves. And yet the hunger persists. There has to be more than simply understanding what you can do well.

Perhaps you have been told or believe that you aren't creative, which also has enormous consequences. It closes a door that to freedom and a far greater story for you and everyone who could benefit from that gift.

Some of our dreams have been met with disinterest. Others with applause. Outwardly, these responses appear to be on opposite ends of the spectrum, yet both have the same foundation. They are tethered to human validation. Over time, we begin to chase the approval of others rather than our original dreams.

Over time, we begin to chase the approval of others rather than our original dreams.

To counter this pull, you have to go back to why you were given your gifts in the first place. It wasn't to win the approval of others. Your specific interests and talents are actually more powerful than that. They offer a gateway to discover your truer identity. And an entirely new way to pursue your dreams.

If God weaves specific talents into each of us, the question is *why*? What is His motive? I believe

He gives each of us a particular calling so He can then spend time with us on that unique playground. This is a way for you and God to get to know each other better as you create together.

Yet clearly something is missing. Because what I just described isn't the way most people pursue their gifting or dreams.

What Fish Can't See

The problem comes when we limit what's possible to what's probable. The first step in seeing with new eyes is to let go of the belief that our current reality is the only reality.

> The first step in seeing with new eyes is to let go of the belief that our current reality is the only reality.

How would you explain the ocean to a goldfish still in his bowl? He was born in a small container with invisible glass walls that define—and limit—his potential. He's a captive who thinks he is free. Swimming circles in his small world has led to small dreams. He thinks the best he can hope for is a bigger bowl when what he needs are bigger dreams. Because an ocean awaits.

What would you see if you could stand outside your current circumstances? Stated another way, who would you be if the world didn't tell you who you are?

> Who would you be if the world didn't tell you who you are?

Though few live from this space, it is possible to walk through each day with a sense of knowing who you are and how that identity connects you to the most important desires, people, and events of your life. You can experience a sense of expectancy in the midst of interruptions, knowing the unplanned can lead to something better than anything you could have planned. Imagine stepping into your relationships and creativity with a power that isn't limited to your solutions or strength?

This is the opposite of what we've been taught since childhood. As children, we naturally gravitated to what brought us joy. But as we grew, we discovered that the way to get ahead was to do what the world (or those we loved) applauded. So we began to pursue our relationships and work according to this matrix. Yet, we eventually realized that something about this approach was wrong. Because the more we based our worth on what we did, the less we became. We shifted from the overachiever to the overwhelmed. Though this cycle may define your world, it doesn't have to remain your world. There is a better way.

What Adventurers Know

Explorers and adventurers understand a great truth. In order to experience the fantastic, they have to first put themselves in fantastic places. It is the same for us.

Conversely, if we rely solely on common sense, we experience a common life.

The last thing we want is more of the status quo. What's needed is an infusion of the fantastical. A shift into something so beyond our dreams that it could only be seen as miraculous.

I'm not suggesting you jump off a cliff and ask God to miraculously provide wings as you fall to the ground. That's not faith. It's foolishness. What I am encouraging you to do is to let go of your preconceived notions of what is possible and ask God about His dreams for you. They will likely be far bigger than anything you've yet imagined. But remember, God will never say anything that goes against what He has already said in Scripture. And especially for large decisions, you want a close circle of strong believers to listen for you as well.

Once you know God is inviting you into more, you have a choice. You can either run with Him or run from Him. In those circumstances, the only way to experience a miracle is to put yourself in a position to need one. That is part of stepping into dreams so big that only God can make them come true.

> The only way to experience a miracle is to put yourself in a position to need one.

But how do we do this?

The Reality of Realms

What if all that has held you back isn't your fault? What if you're simply living in the wrong realm? We all spend our lives in one of two places. We can't alternate from one to the other, like trying on a new pair of clothes. The two are actually in fierce opposition to each other.

Your realm is the place where you exist. It colors how you interpret everything about your life. It's your outlook or perspective. It affects how you see yourself and how others feel when they are around you. It influences what you pursue and what pursues you. It has huge impact on your identity and your imagination. Each realm even has its own language of bondage or freedom.

This explains why people react so differently in similar circumstances. Yes, it's partially due to who they are. But who they are is shaped by the realm they live in. The bad news is we all begin in the wrong realm. The good news is we don't have to stay there. We get to choose where we exist.

Your realm is the place where you exist. It colors how you interpret everything about your life.

The Shift to "With"

In the first realm, we live and pursue life as if it were all up to us. Whether we fail or succeed, we do it in our own strength. That means we only have ourselves to blame or to credit. It is a place of doing more—because we're evaluated on what we do. I call this the Orphan Realm and I was a long-term resident there.

Those who live in this place go through life overwhelmed, disheartened, and isolated. In other words: alone. Our bosses, our leaders, and even our spouses convey (often unintentionally) that the way to *be* more is to *do* more. Yet the more we give, the more is demanded of us. We end up losing ourselves in the expectations of others. We realize no matter how much we give, it is never enough. The path we thought would be satisfying eventually sucks the marrow from our weary bones.

You can believe in God and still miss life with Him. You can know about God and still live as an Orphan.

You can believe in God and still miss life with Him. You can know about God and still live as an Orphan.

The goal isn't just to escape what isn't working, it's to be free from that way of living. The foundational shift requires moving from a life of independence and self-reliance to a life wholly dependent on God.

I understand how this may sound passive if you're used to making things happen. Yet it is actually an extremely courageous decision that invites you into an unscripted life without limits. God sees farther and better than you. Why not run with Him instead of alone in the dark?

Living with a dependence on God and not on yourself is only available in the second realm—a place where we pursue our life, love, and creativity *with* God. I've named this the Freedom Realm. We will discover more about this realm as we continue on our journey.

The Invitation

God has turned my world upside down in the most counterintuitive ways. He's shown me the futility of trying to make life work on my own. As Scottish poet and novelist George MacDonald (1824–1905) notes: "In whatever a man does without God, he must fail miserably—or succeed more miserably."[1]

Life *without* God leads to misery. The key is relationship. Yet so many who believe in God miss the experience of life *with* Him.

Life *without* God leads to misery. The key is relationship. Yet so many who believe in God miss the experience of life *with* Him.

As I allowed God to father me, He gave me a new life mission: pursue the hearts of those living like orphans and awaken them to their core identity as His sons and daughters.

That is why I've written this book. I could have filled it with facts and formulas. But doing so would bore both of us. So instead, I'd like to tell you a story.

Just as explorers travel to fantastical places in search of the unknown, stories can transport us to places where we can then see our own stories more clearly. They invite us into other worlds and, in the process, offer a new way of seeing our own world.

Stories speak to our hearts in ways that facts alone fall short. Like when tears come unexpectedly while watching a movie. Or when a song you haven't heard in a decade provokes a forgotten longing.

We underestimate stories when we see them as

just an escape from reality or a vehicle to teach a lesson. We don't need to escape our lives—nor do we need more lessons. We need our hearts awakened. And nothing reaches the heart faster than story.

So rather than offer more theories or principles, I give you this story. Like a meal worth savoring, we'll pause after each chapter for you to catch your breath and consider what's going on at a heart level.

For too long, we've lived without hopes and dreams. There is a better way.

It is the story of *with*.

Printed in Great Britain
by Amazon

56589870R00185